Preparing for School Leadership in Texas

Mastering Principal Competencies

and

Challenges of 21ˢᵗ Century Leadership

by

Kriss Kemp-Graham

NCPEA Publications

National Council of Professors of Educational Administration

Ypsilanti, Michigan

Published by NCPEA Publications
The publications of the National Council of Professors of Educational Administration (NCPEA)
http://www.ncpeapublications.org

Printed in United States of America
Library of Congress Cataloging-in-Publication Data

Kemp-Graham, Kriss
Preparing for school leadership in Texas: Mastering principal competencies and challenges of 21st century leadership
ISBN 978-1-4951-1151-8 (pbk)

How to order this book:
NCPEA Press, a book publisher for NCPEA Publications, offers *Preparing for School Leadership in Texas* as a Print-on-Demand hard copy and as an eBook at: www.ncpeapublication.org Books are prepared in Perfect Bound binding and delivery is 3-5 business days. eBooks are available upon ordering and delivered electronically in minutes to one's computer or other electronic reading devise.

NCPEA Executive Director   James E. Berry
NCPEA Press Director and Production Editor   Theodore B. Creighton
NCPEA Publications Director and Technical Editor   Brad E. Bizzell
Cover Design   Brad E. Bizzell

Contents

Note: With the purchase of this book in either print copy or eBook copy, you have free access to the author's PowerPoint presentations that accompany Chapters 2-10. These presentations can be downloaded from the web link: http://www.ncpeapublications.org/files/2PrBUgHX9PrJvDq.zip

CHAPTER 1
Introduction: Finally, "A Leadership Practice Field"

A "practice" is an activity that you do repeatedly to achieve a particular experience or outcome. For example, students of sports (e.g., tennis or basketball), music (e.g., violin or piano), and medicine (e.g., internships) spend hours and hours practicing. This practice has a deliberate design and intention, that, when used well, produces a defined result: competitive skill, musical accuracy and interpretation, and the ability to perform medical diagnosis and treatment.

I can think of no other profession that fails to value or provide sufficient opportunities for new professionals to practice—in a different kind of space where one can practice and learn. The medical field has a *practice field*, musicians and dancers have a *practice field*, the Miami Heat have a *practice field*, pilots and astronauts have a *practice field*, and on and on—but do we have a *practice field* in school administration? I argue that we do not—and the internship as we know it suffers from relevancy and quality. Murphy (1999) reported that although supervised practice could be the most critical phase of the administrator's preparation, the component is notoriously weak. Murphy further claims that field-based practices do not involve an adequate number of experiences and are arranged on the basis of convenience.

For some time I have argued for the implementation of a "leadership practice field" into our preparation programs. The conceptual notion at work here is that of creating a bridge between a performance field (working *in* the system) and a practice field (working *on* the system). This model is based on the work of Daniel Kim, colleague of Peter Senge (*The Fifth Discipline)* and cofounder of the MIT Organizational Learning Center, where he is the director of the Learning Laboratory Research Project. The central idea is that a leadership practice field provides an environment where a prospective leader can experiment with alternative strategies and policies, test assumptions, and practice working through the complex issues of leadership in a constructive and productive manner (Kim, 1995).

Kim is fond of using the following scenario as an introduction to the "practice field" concept:

> *Imagine you are walking across a tightrope stretched between two skyscraper buildings in Chicago. The wind is blowing and the rope is shaking as you inch your way forward. One of your teammates sits in the wheelbarrow you are balancing in front of you, while another colleague sits on your shoulders. There are no safety nets, no harnesses. You think to yourself, "one false move and the three of us will take an express elevator straight down to the street." Suddenly your trainer yells from the other side, "Try a new move! Experiment! Take some risks! Remember, you are a learning team!"* (Kim, 1995, p. 353)

Kim continues by admitting the ludicrous nature of this scenario, but realizes that this is precisely what many companies expect their management teams to do—experiment and learn in an environment that is risky, turbulent, and unpredictable. And unlike musicians, medical students, or sports teams, management teams do not have an adequate practice field; they are nearly always on the performance field.

I suggest this scenario truly resembles the life of school principals, and the concept of a practice field is applicable to the field of educational administration and especially its preparation programs. Except for a brief experience with some form of internship, notoriously considered weak and suffering from a lack of quality and relevance, where do prospective school leaders get the opportunity to leave the pressures of day-to-day teaching and/or administration and enter a different kind of space where they can practice and learn?

When practicing a symphony, the conductor can have the orchestra *slow down* the tempo in order to practice certain sections. A medical student in residence has the opportunity to *slow down* and practice certain medical procedures and diagnoses. The Miami Heat spend most of their time in a practice field, *slowing down the tempo* and practicing certain moves, strategies, and assumptions. All of these practice fields exist in an environment with opportunities for making mistakes, in a "safe-failing space" to enhance learning. Aspiring new principals need the opportunity to *slow down the tempo* and practice certain moves and aspects of their jobs.

Author and former school administrator Kriss Kemp-Graham has developed and created such a space with this new and welcome book, *Preparing for School Leadership in Texas: Mastering Principal Competencies and Challenges of 21st Century Leadership*. Though targeted around the Texas Principal Competencies, I will be encouraging her to consider a sequel that focuses on the national perspective as well.

You, as practicing principals and professors of preparation programs continue to tell us that what you do in your jobs in schools bears little resemblance to the Internship preparation received at the university. You also share your frustration with having so little time to be proactive—you are constantly required to be reactive. I wrote in a book, *Leading from Below the Surface* in 2005 (Corwin Press) that I was not optimistic about *when* university preparation programs would implement "leadership practice fields." Yes, since then there has been some limited progress with simulated activity programs, but not until now has there been such a blueprint to follow and such a genuine and effective approach to helping perspective school leaders to close the gap between their conceptual belief of the right course of action and what they will actually choose to do in the real situation.

NCPEA Press and NCPEA Publications are proud to publish Kemp-Graham's "practice field." We also believe that through more practice, prospective leaders discover that sometimes conflict and confrontation are OK and can be positive and productive. And, we grow professionally by developing tolerance for diversity, honest disagreements, and healthy debate.

Theodore Creighton
Director, NCPEA Press

Creighton, T. (2005). *Leading from below the surface.* Thousand Oaks, CA: Corwin Press.
Kim, D. (1995). Managerial practice fields: Infrastructures of a learning organization. In S. Chawla & J. Renesh (Eds.), *Learning organizations: Developing cultures for tomorrow's workplace* (pp. 351-363). Portland Oregon: Productivity Press.

CHAPTER 2
TeXes Principal Competency 1

(Photo: 2D MAW, Sgt. Samuel R. Beyers http://www.defenseimagery.mil/imageRetrieve.action?guid=33f2fd2c52f7ca7189e88c8ea1f39ae324622f3b&t=2 25 August 2010)

Congratulations! I am pleased to inform you that you have been appointed as the Principal of Joy Elementary School. It is with great pleasure that I share with you that your appointment has been affirmed by the full support and vote of confidence of our school board, community members, parents and students. As the new Principal of Joy Elementary we are confident that you will bring a renewed vision and commitment to the students and faculty.

Joy Elementary is not without its share of challenges however, your demonstrated commitment to the education of all children and your enthusiasm and willingness to work effortlessly to transform Joy Elementary School from a struggling school to a high achieving school is exactly the type of vision and leadership that is needed at Joy. Joy Elementary has experienced numerous changes in administration and faculty that has resulted in a culture of mediocrity. The shaping of Joy's campus culture by facilitating the development, articulation, implementation, and stewardship of a vision of learning that is shared and supported by the school community should be a top priority.

As was shared with you during your final interview, we believe in transparency, collaboration and strong school community partnerships. In keeping with our traditions and commitment to a culture of transparency, community and family engagement, a community meet and greet has already been scheduled for you to fellowship with your new school family. During this event you will be expected to articulate your implementation plan for the re-envisioning of Joy Elementary School. Present at this meeting will be school board members, your staff, community, central office staff, parents, students and elected officials. Once again, congratulations, I wish you much success!

Dr. Jane J. Transformation
Superintendent
Heaven ISD

RE-IMAGINING JOY ELEMENTARY

Joy elementary is located in Heaven, Texas a small rural community of less than 10,000 residents. The major employer in Joy is Walmart. The average family income is $14,000. After the saw mill and tire factories closed two years ago due to the recession, the unemployment rate in Heaven rose to three times the state rate. In fact, small businesses were so adversely impacted by the recession that more than 80% of Heaven's economic base has disappeared. Businesses remaining are a gas station, donut shop, Chinese food restaurant, dry cleaners, small family owned grocery store, medical office, and Walmart.

In the last three years there have been five Principals and three Assistant Principals. The staff mobility rate is higher than the student mobility rate. On any given day, there are at least five substitute teachers in the building, teachers appear to be accident prone, during the last five years, at least three teachers have fallen under suspicious circumstances. Approximately 10% of the teachers are out on a leave of absence—medical, personal, family or unpaid; another 20% have chronic illnesses that require them to miss work intermittently per federal FMLA. The school has been rated academically unacceptable for over 6 years. Every teacher at Joy has been rated exceeds expectations or proficient on their performance evaluations for the last decade.

Your first task as the new Principal of Joy Elementary will be to create a Power Point presentation outlining your plan to re-shape the campus culture. You will be presenting this Power Point to the entire school community. Joy Elementary School is in need of extreme REVISIONING. It is essential that you review all of the artifacts presented in this case study. Your PowerPoint Presentation must demonstrate that you have the understanding and the ability to:

1. Create a campus culture that sets high expectations, promotes learning, and provides intellectual stimulation for self, students, and staff.
2. Ensure that parents and other members of the community are an integral part of the campus culture.
3. Implement strategies to ensure the development of collegial relationships and effective collaboration.
4. Respond appropriately to diverse needs in shaping the campus culture.
5. Use various types of information (e.g., demographic data, campus climate inventory results, student achievement data, emerging issues affecting education) to develop a campus vision and create a plan for implementing the vision.
6. Use strategies for involving all stakeholders in planning processes to enable the collaborative development of a shared campus vision focused on teaching and learning.
7. Facilitate the collaborative development of a plan that clearly articulates objectives and strategies for implementing a campus vision.
8. Align financial, human, and material resources to support implementation of a campus vision.
9. Establish procedures to assess and modify implementation plans to ensure achievement of the campus vision.
10. Support innovative thinking and risk taking within the school community and view unsuccessful experiences as learning opportunities.
11. Acknowledge and celebrate the contributions of students, staff, parents, and community members toward the realization of the campus vision.

Hint: Each artifact included in this case study represents a challenge that you must address in your plan.

'The true leader senses and transforms the needs of followers.'
James McGregor Burns

TEXAS EDUCATION AGENCY
Accountability Summary
Joy Elementary

Accountability Rating

Improvement Required

Met Standards on	Did Not Meet Standards on
- Student Achievement	- Closing Performance Gaps
- Student Progress	

Performance Index Report

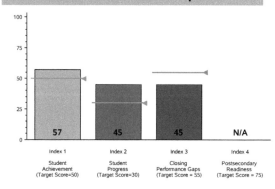

Index 1	Index 2	Index 3	Index 4
57	45	45	N/A
Student Achievement (Target Score=50)	Student Progress (Target Score=30)	Closing Performance Gaps (Target Score = 55)	Postsecondary Readiness (Target Score = 75)

Performance Index Summary

Index	Points Earned	Maximum Points	Index Score
1 - Student Achievement	285	504	57
2 - Student Progress	543	1,200	45
3 - Closing Performance Gaps	316	700	45
4 - Postsecondary Readiness	N/A	N/A	N/A

Distinction Designation

Academic Achievement in Reading/ELA

Percent of Eligible Measures in Top Quartile
1 out of 4 = 25%

DOES NOT QUALIFY

Academic Achievement in Mathematics

Percent of Eligible Measures in Top Quartile
0 out of 3 = 0%

DOES NOT QUALIFY

Top 25 Percent Student Progress

DOES NOT QUALIFY

Campus Demographics

Campus Type	Elementary
Campus Size	550 Students
Grade Span	PK - 05
Percent Economically Disadvantaged	97.3%
Percent English Language Learners	50.9%
Mobility Rate	21.7%

System Safeguards

Number and Percent of Indicators Met

Performance Rates	13 out of 19 = 68%
Participation Rates	10 out of 10 = 100%
Graduation Rates	N/A
Total	**23 out of 29 = 79%**

School Campus: Joy Elementary

	General Fund	%	Per Student	All Funds	%	Per Student
Expenditures by Object (Objects 6100-6600)						
Total Expenditures	3,155,794	100.00	5,576	3,792,818	100.00	6,701
Operating-Payroll	2,902,278	91.97	5,128	3,265,090	86.09	5,769
Other Operating	251,981	7.98	445	526,193	13.87	930
Non-Operating(Equipt/Supplies)	1,535	0.05	3	1,535	0.04	3
Expenditures by Function (Objects 6100-6400 Only)						
Total Operating Expenditures	3,154,259	100.00	5,573	3,791,283	100.00	6,698
Instruction (11,95) *	2,271,941	72.03	4,014	2,508,739	66.17	4,432
Instructional Res/Media (12) *	88,740	2.81	157	88,740	2.34	157
Curriculum/Staff Develop (13) *	1,535	0.05	3	1,535	0.04	3
Instructional Leadership (21) *	53,625	1.70	95	53,625	1.41	95
School Leadership (23) *	263,324	8.35	465	263,324	6.95	465
Guidance/Counseling Svcs (31) *	118,829	3.77	210	118,829	3.13	210
Social Work Services (32) *	0	0.00	0	0	0.00	0
Health Services (33) *	70,741	2.24	125	70,741	1.87	125
Food (35) **	0	0.00	0	390,184	10.29	689
Extracurricular (36) *	0	0.00	0	0	0.00	0
Plant Maint/Operation (51) * **	251,174	7.96	444	257,821	6.80	456
Security/Monitoring (52) * **	0	0.00	0	0	0.00	0
Data Processing Svcs (53)* **	0	0.00	0	0	0.00	0
Program expenditures by Program (Objects 6100-6400 only)						
Total Operating Expenditures	2,762,870	100.00	4,881	3,003,063	100.00	5,306
Regular	2,346,731	84.94	4,146	2,347,031	78.15	4,147
Gifted & Talented	0	0.00	0	0	0.00	0
Career & Technical	0	0.00	0	0	0.00	0
Students with Disabilities	2,865	0.10	5	58,637	1.95	104
Accelerated Education	0	0.00	0	6,817	0.23	12
Bilingual	2,865	0.10	5	58,637	1.95	104
Nondisc Alted-AEP Basic Serv	0	0.00	0	0	0.00	0
Disc Alted-DAEP Basic Serv	0	0.00	0	0	0.00	0
Disc Alted-DAEP Supplemental	0	0.00	0	0	0.00	0
T1 A Schoolwide-St Comp >=40%	235,093	8.51	415	423,960	14.12	749
Athletic Programming	0	0.00	0	0	0.00	0
High School Allotment	0	0.00	0	0	0.00	0

*

Note: Some amounts may not total due to rounding.

TEXAS EDUCATION AGENCY
Index 1: Student Achievement Data Table
Joy Elementary

STAAR Performance	All Students	African American	Hispanic	White	American Indian	Asian	Pacific Islander	Two or More Races	Special Ed	Econ Disadv	ELL
All Subjects											
Percent of Tests											
% at Phase-in 1 Level II or above	57%	**	66%	*	-	-	-	-	24%	56%	69%
% at Final Level II or above	19%	**	24%	*	-	-	-	-	7%	19%	28%
% at Level III Advanced	8%	**	12%	*	-	-	-	-	0%	8%	14%
Number of Tests											
# at Phase-in 1 Level II or above	285	**	198	*	-	-	-	-	7	274	158
# at Final Level II or above	94	**	71	*	-	-	-	-	2	91	64
# at Level III Advanced	39	**	36	*	-	-	-	-	0	37	32
Total Tests	504	**	301	*	-	-	-	-	29	489	230
Reading											
Percent of Tests											
% at Phase-in 1 Level II or above	61%	**	70%	*	-	-	-	-	*	59%	75%
% at Final Level II or above	18%	**	26%	*	-	-	-	-	*	18%	32%
% at Level III Advanced	8%	**	13%	*	-	-	-	-	*	8%	17%
Number of Tests											
# at Phase-in 1 Level II or above	109	**	73	*	-	-	-	-	*	104	58
# at Final Level II or above	33	**	27	*	-	-	-	-	*	32	25
# at Level III Advanced	15	**	14	*	-	-	-	-	*	14	13
Total Tests	180	**	104	*	-	-	-	-	*	175	77
Mathematics											
Percent of Tests											
% at Phase-in 1 Level II or above	58%	**	71%	*	-	-	-	-	*	58%	75%
% at Final Level II or above	20%	**	27%	*	-	-	-	-	*	20%	32%
% at Level III Advanced	11%	**	17%	*	-	-	-	-	*	10%	21%
Number of Tests											
# at Phase-in 1 Level II or above	104	**	74	*	-	-	-	-	*	101	58
# at Final Level II or above	36	**	28	*	-	-	-	-	*	35	25
# at Level III Advanced	19	**	18	*	-	-	-	-	*	18	16
Total Tests	180	**	104	*	-	-	-	-	*	175	77
Writing											
Percent of Tests											
% at Phase-in 1 Level II or above	57%	50%	61%	-	-	-	-	-	*	58%	66%
% at Final Level II or above	21%	21%	20%	-	-	-	-	-	*	21%	20%
% at Level III Advanced	4%	0%	6%	-	-	-	-	-	*	4%	5%
Number of Tests											
# at Phase-in 1 Level II or above	47	14	33	-	-	-	-	-	*	45	29
# at Final Level II or above	17	6	11	-	-	-	-	-	*	16	9
# at Level III Advanced	3	0	3	-	-	-	-	-	*	3	2
Total Tests	82	28	54	-	-	-	-	-	*	78	44

'*' Indicates results are masked due to small numbers to protect student confidentiality.

'**' When only one ethnic/race group is masked, then the second smallest ethnic/race group is masked (regardless of size).

'-' Indicates there are no students in the group.

TEXAS EDUCATION AGENCY
Index 2: Student Progress Data Table
Joy Elementary

	All Students	African American	Hispanic	White	American Indian	Asian	Pacific Islander	Two or More Races	Special Ed	ELL
Reading										
Number of Tests	127	46	81	-	-	-	-	-	*	64
# Met or Exceeded Progress	86	27	59	-	-	-	-	-	*	50
# Exceeded Progress	24	6	18	-	-	-	-	-	*	17
% Met or Exceeded Progress	68%	59%	73%	-	-	-	-	-	*	78%
% Exceeded Progress	19%	13%	22%	-	-	-	-	-	*	27%
Mathematics										
Number of Tests	64	46	18	-	-	-	-	-	*	*
# Met or Exceeded Progress	44	30	14	-	-	-	-	-	*	*
# Exceeded Progress	18	10	8	-	-	-	-	-	*	*
% Met or Exceeded Progress	69%	65%	78%	-	-	-	-	-	*	*
% Exceeded Progress	28%	22%	44%	-	-	-	-	-	*	*
Writing										
Number of Tests	-	-	-	-	-	-	-	-	-	-
# Met or Exceeded Progress	-	-	-	-	-	-	-	-	-	-
# Exceeded Progress	-	-	-	-	-	-	-	-	-	-
% Met or Exceeded Progress	-	-	-	-	-	-	-	-	-	-
% Exceeded Progress	-	-	-	-	-	-	-	-	-	-

SURVEY RESPONSES FROM TEACHERS

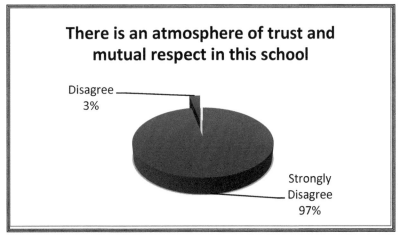

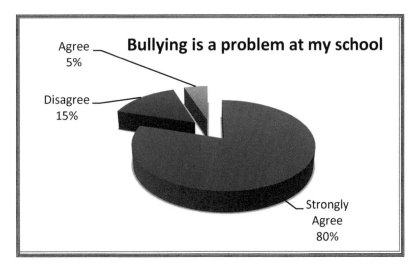

SURVEY RESPONSES FROM TEACHERS

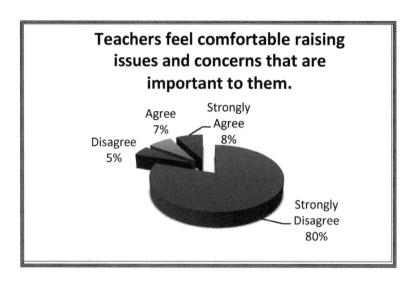

Teachers feel comfortable raising issues and concerns that are important to them.

Agree 7%
Strongly Agree 8%
Disagree 5%
Strongly Disagree 80%

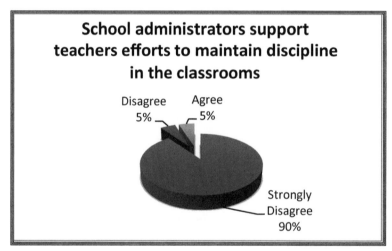

School administrators support teachers efforts to maintain discipline in the classrooms

Disagree 5%
Agree 5%
Strongly Disagree 90%

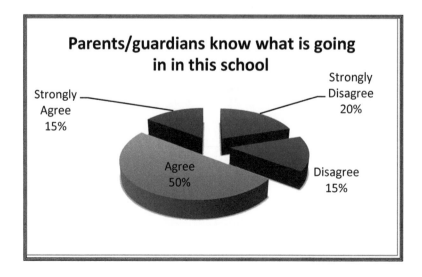

Parents/guardians know what is going in in this school

Strongly Agree 15%
Strongly Disagree 20%
Agree 50%
Disagree 15%

SURVEY RESPONSES FROM TEACHERS

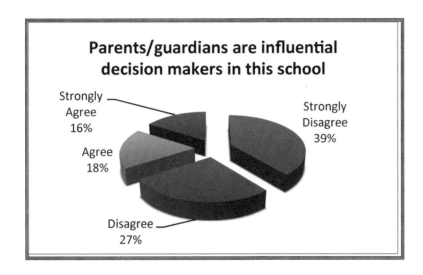

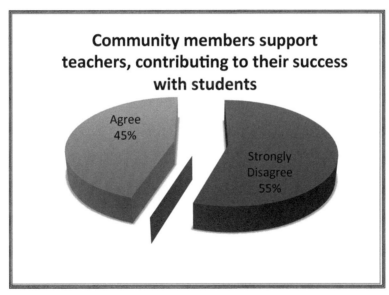

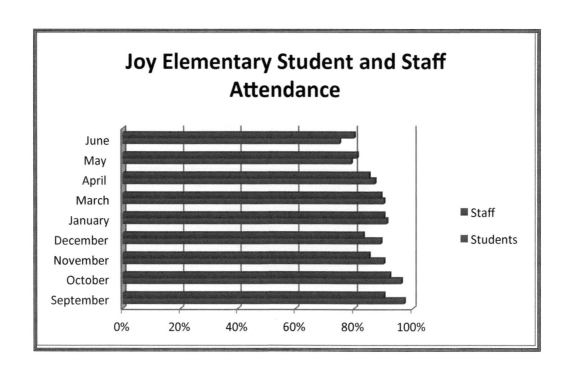

Joy Elementary Student and Staff Attendance

	Strongly Disagree	Disagree	Agree	Strongly Agree
Teachers assign high-quality homework that helps my child learn.	40%	28%	30%	2%
I like my child's school building	75%	5%	10%	10%
The learning environment at this school is excellent	55%	25%	15%	5%
My child feels safe at this school	80%	20%	0%	0%
Communication with families occurs in an open and respectful manner	95%	5%	0%	0%
Students at my child's school are well behaved.	50%	25%	15%	10%
The teachers at this school are excellent	75%	5%	15%	5%
Teachers at this school set high standards	60%	0%	30%	10%
I respect the schools teachers	80%	0%	15%	5%
I am satisfied with this school	70%	30%	0%	0%
I am proud my child attends this school	90%	10%	0%	0%

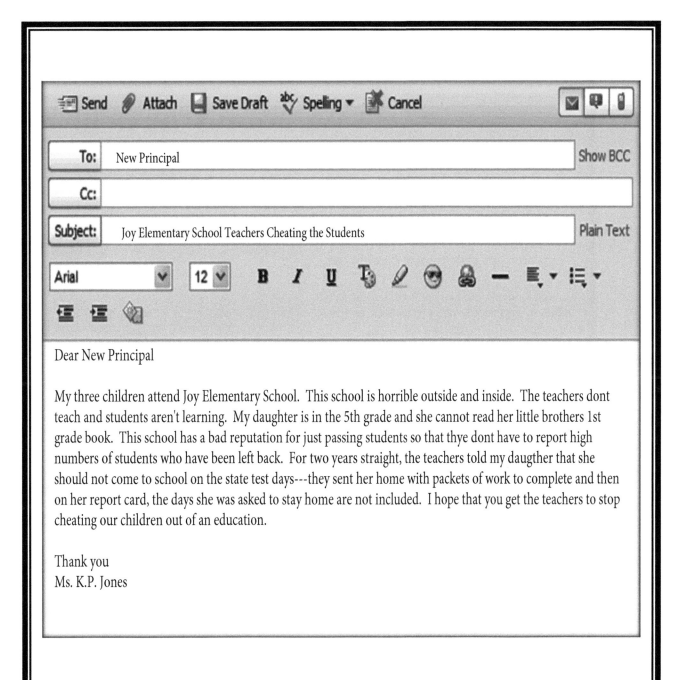

Send   Attach   Save Draft   Spelling ▼   Cancel

To:	New Principal	Show BCC
Cc:		
Subject:	Joy Elementary School Teachers Cheating the Students	Plain Text

Arial   12   **B** *I* U

Dear New Principal

My three children attend Joy Elementary School. This school is horrible outside and inside. The teachers dont teach and students aren't learning. My daughter is in the 5th grade and she cannot read her little brothers 1st grade book. This school has a bad reputation for just passing students so that thye dont have to report high numbers of students who have been left back. For two years straight, the teachers told my daugther that she should not come to school on the state test days---they sent her home with packets of work to complete and then on her report card, the days she was asked to stay home are not included. I hope that you get the teachers to stop cheating our children out of an education.

Thank you
Ms. K.P. Jones

Teacher Self Perception of Culturally Competent Practices

■ Frequently   ■ Occasionally   ■ Rarely

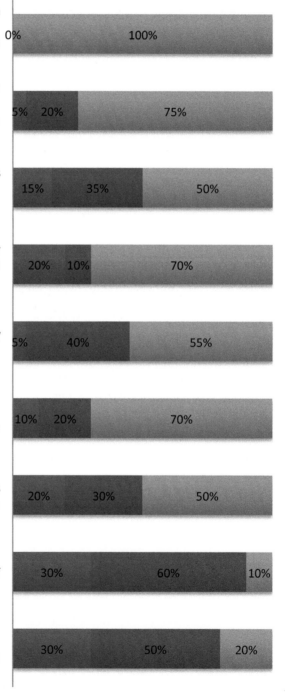

Before making a home visit, I seek information on acceptable behaviors, courtesies,customs, and expectations that are unique to the culturally and ethnically diverse groups served in our school.
0% | 100%

I seek information from students, families or key community resources that will assist in curriculum/instruction adaptation to respond to the needs and preferences of culturally and
5% 20% | 75%

I understand that the perception of education has different meanings to different cultural or ethnic groups.
15% 35% | 50%

I understand that religion and other beliefs may influence how students and individuals respond to traditional education.
20% 10% | 70%

I recognize that the value of education may vary greatly among cultures
5% 40% | 55%

I ensure directly or indirectly (by reminding administration or other staff) that information sent home takes into account the average literacy levels and language of the students and families
10% 20% | 70%

When using videos, films or other media resources, I ensure that they reflect the cultures and ethnic background of students and families served by our school.
20% 30% | 50%

I ensure that magazines, brochures, and other printed materials reflect the different cultures of students and families served by our school.
30% 60% 10%

I display pictures, posters, artwork and other décor that reflect the cultures and ethnic backgrounds of students and families served by our school.
30% 50% 20%

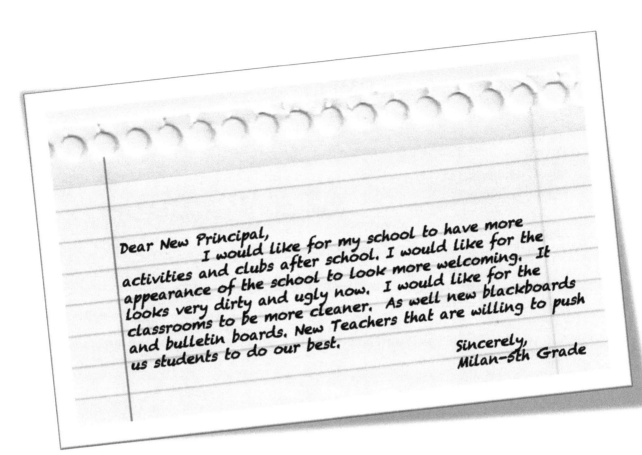

Dear New Principal,
I would like for my school to have more activities and clubs after school. I would like for the appearance of the school to look more welcoming. It looks very dirty and ugly now. I would like for the classrooms to be more cleaner. As well new blackboards and bulletin boards. New Teachers that are willing to push us students to do our best.

Sincerely,
Milan-5th Grade

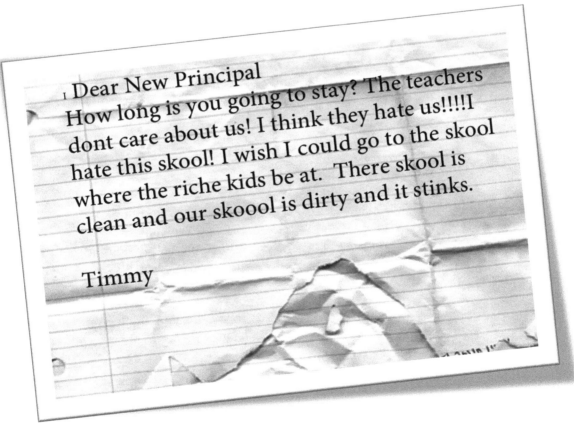

Dear New Principal
How long is you going to stay? The teachers dont care about us! I think they hate us!!!!I hate this skool! I wish I could go to the skool where the riche kids be at. There skool is clean and our skoool is dirty and it stinks.

Timmy

SUPPLEMENTARY RESOURCES
CHAPTER TWO
COMPETENCY ONE

Books

Passing the Principal TExES Exam: Keys to Certification and School Leadership
Elaine Wilmore

Shaping School Culture: Pitfalls, Paradoxes, and Promises
Terrence E. Deal (Author), Kent D. Peterson (Author)

Leverage Leadership: A Practical Guide to Building Exceptional Schools
Paul Bambrick-Santoyo (Author)

101 Mission Statements from Top Companies: Plus Guidelines for Writing Your Own
Mission Statement
Jeffrey Abrahams (Author)

The Naked Presenter: Delivering Powerful Presentations With or Without Slides (Voices
That Matter)
by Garr Reynolds (Author)

Articles

Kose, B. W. (2011). Developing a Transformative School Vision: Lessons From Peer-
Nominated Principals. *Education & Urban Society*, *43*(2), 119-136.
doi:10.1177/0013124510380231

Merz, A. H., & Swim, T. (2011). 'You can't mandate what matters': bumping visions
against practices. *Teacher Development*, *15*(3), 305-318.
doi:10.1080/13664530.2011.608512

Bottoms, G., & Schmidt-Davis, J. (2010). The Three Essentials: Improving Schools
Requires District Vision, District and State Support, and Principal Leadership. *Southern
Regional Education Board (SREB)*.http://www.wallacefoundation.org/knowledge-
center/school-leadership/district-policy-and-practice/Documents/Three-Essentials-to-
Improving-Schools.pdf

Moolenaar, N. M., Daly, A. J., & Sleegers, P. J. (2010). Occupying the principal position:
Examining relationships between transformational leadership, social network position,
and schools' innovative climate. *Educational administration quarterly*, *46*(5), 623-670.

Tschannen-Moran, M., & Tschannen-Moran, B. (2011). Taking a strengths-based focus improves school climate. *Journal of School Leadership*, *21*(3), 422-448.

Cohen, J., McCabe, L., Michelli, N. M., & Pickeral, T. (2009). School climate: Research, policy, practice, and teacher education. *The Teachers College Record*, *111*(1), 180-213.

Gruenert, S. (2008). School culture, school climate: They are not the same thing. *PRINCIPAL-ARLINGTON-*, *87*(4), 56.http://www.naesp.org/resources/2/Principal/2008/M-Ap56.pdf

Websites and Blogs
http://principalspov.blogspot.com/p/effective-leadership.html
http://georgecouros.ca/blog/archives/tag/positive-school-culture
http://www.schoolculture.net
http://centerforschoolchange.org/publications/minnesota-charter-school-handbook/vision-and-mission/
http://www.educationworld.com/a_admin/admin/admin229.shtml
http://www.communityschools.org/scalingup/
http://www.csos.jhu.edu/p2000/center.htm

Mini Projects
Re-write the mission and vision statement. Present your plan for involving all key school stakeholders in this process.

Create a PowerPoint Presentation where you present to your school community your plan for community engagement.

You have received a grant to hire a community engagement staff member. Write the job announcement and job description.

Your superintendent has allocated $500,000 to your school to help with school improvement. Create a spending plan that is aligned to your school mission and vision.

You have been invited by the school PTA to speak at their annual diversity dinner, write the speech that you will deliver.

Write an open letter to parents in your school community about your commitment to diversity. Write a plan for the dissemination of this open letter.

Write an introductory letter to your staff which would include your views on culture, climate, academic achievement, diversity and your goals for the school.

Create your first month's calendar. Record what you plan to do and who you plan to meet with.

Discussion/Reflection Topics

1. 'Some schools develop 'toxic' cultures which actively discourage efforts to improve teaching or student achievement.' **Deal and Patterson**

2. "A school's culture has more influence on life and learning in the schoolhouse than the president of the country, the state department of education, the superintendent, the school board, or even the principal, teachers, and parents can ever have.-Roland Barth

3. "Vision is the art of seeing what is invisible to others." Jonathan Swift

4. Vision without action is merely a dream. Action without vision just passes the time. Vision with action can change the world." Joel A. Barker

5. "Vision without action is a daydream. Action with without vision is a nightmare." **- Japanese Proverb**

6. "Leadership is the capacity to translate vision into reality." **- Warren Bennis**

7. The very essence of leadership is that you have a vision. It's got to be a vision you articulate clearly and forcefully on every occasion. You can't blow an uncertain trumpet." **- Theodore Hesburgh**

8. "Vision animates, inspires, transforms purpose into action." **- Warren Bennis**

9. The best way to predict the future is to create it." **- Alan Kay**

10. "Management has a lot to do with answers. Leadership is a function of questions. And the first question for a leader always is: 'Who do we intend to be?' Not 'What are we going to do?' but 'Who do we intend to be?' **- Max DePree**

11. You don't lead by pointing and telling people some place to go. You lead by going to that place and making a case." **- Ken Kesey**

12. Great teachers set high standards for all their students, not just the ones who are already achieving...Yet [they also] establish...an atmosphere of genuine affection and concern.. Barth, R., The Culture Builder

CHAPTER 3
TeXes Principal Competency 2

9

Berlitz Independent School District
732909 INTERNATIONAL Drive
Rosetta Stone, Texas 75390

Congratulations! Félicitations!, Вітаємо, поздравления

I am pleased to inform you that you have made it to the final phase of the principal selection process for the Alexander Graham Bell School of Communication, Language and Cultures. The Bell school is our very own United Nations. We have over 400 students, representing every continent across the World. There are more than 10 languages spoken at Bell and for approximately 90 percent of our students, English is not the primary language spoken in their homes. Throughout our extensive Principal selection process, you demonstrated an extraordinary commitment to communicating and collaborating with all members of the school community, responding to diverse interests and needs, and mobilizing resources to promote student success. Our students' needs are as diverse as the student population. Students and their families at Bell are faced with many of the same issues that schools across Texas are being required to address.

This last phase of the selection process will require you to complete an "in basket" activity to demonstrate how well you are able to communicate and collaborate with school stakeholders to promote student success. You will be presented with several issues that you will need to respond to. Your task will be to develop a communications/community relations plan that addresses the following:

- New TEA Accountability School Rating System
- School Budget
- Improved School/Community Communications about student progress and school activities
- School activities and programs that are inclusive of all people and cultures.

To assist you with this task you will be provided with several artifacts that will provide background information on each of these issues as well as school and community demographics that will help you to better plan effective strategies for communicating your responses to the diverse community of the Bell School. It is important to remember that there are numerous communication venues that will allow for effective communication beyond traditional notes home from school. Be creative and remember the diverse community that you will be serving.

You will be presenting your recommendations to a committee of 30 persons that will be comprised of school board members, parents, teachers, clergy, students and community members. Your presentation has been scheduled for the third Saturday of this month. Please make us aware of any technology that you will need for this presentation. Once again, congratulations! I look forward to your presentation.

Dr. Paul Angle
Superintendent

ALEXANDER GRAHAM BELL SCHOOL OF COMMUNICATION, LANGUAGE AND CULTURE

Alexander Graham Bell School is located in a mid-sized town in Berlitz, Texas. Just 20 minutes from downtown Houston north of IH-30, surrounded by more than 50 miles of shoreline on beautiful Lake Ray Thomas, and home to over 57,000 residents, Berlitz is "On the Water, and On the Move!" Berlitz is ranked in the Top 25 "Best Places To Live" by Money Magazine and was designated the "#1 mid-sized town in America to Move to" by Movoto!

Key to "wowing" the search committee and landing this job will be your ability to assess and respond to the issues presented in this case while being cognizant of the internal and external needs of the school community. More specifically, keeping in mind, the various political, social and economic issues that the community is faced with—your presentation should be reflective of and sensitive to these very special needs. The candidate chosen as the Principal for this school will demonstrate an outstanding ability to do the following:

•Communicate effectively with families and other community members in varied educational contexts.

•Apply skills for building consensus and managing conflict.

•Implement effective strategies for systematically communicating with and gathering input from all campus stakeholders.

•Develop and implement strategies for effective internal and external communications.

•Develop and implement a comprehensive program of community relations that effectively involves and informs multiple constituencies, including the media.

•Provide varied and meaningful opportunities for parents/caregivers to be engaged in the education of their children.

•Establish partnerships with parents/caregivers, businesses, and others in the community to strengthen programs and support campus goals.

•Communicate and work effectively with diverse groups in the school community to ensure that all students have an equal opportunity for educational success.

• Respond to pertinent political, social, and economic issues in the internal and external environment

TEXAS EDUCATION AGENCY
Accountability Summary
Alexander Graham Bell Elementary
School

Accountability Rating

Met Standard

Met Standards on	Did Not Meet Standards on
- Student Achievement	- NONE
- Student Progress	
- Closing Performance Gaps	

Distinction Designation

Academic Achievement in Reading/ELA
Percent of Eligible Measures in Top Quartile 2 out of 4 = 50%
DISTINCTION EARNED

Academic Achievement in Mathematics
Percent of Eligible Measures in Top Quartile 2 out of 3 = 67%
DISTINCTION EARNED

Top 25 Percent Student Progress
DISTINCTION EARNED

Performance Index Report

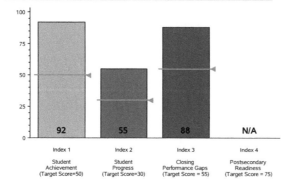

	Index 1	Index 2	Index 3	Index 4
	92	55	88	N/A
	Student Achievement (Target Score=50)	Student Progress (Target Score=30)	Closing Performance Gaps (Target Score = 55)	Postsecondary Readiness (Target Score = 75)

Campus Demographics

Campus Type	Elementary
Campus Size	420 Students
Grade Span	PK - 05
Percent Economically Disadvantaged	25.0%
Percent English Language Learners	27.9%
Mobility Rate	8.5%

Performance Index Summary

Index	Points Earned	Maximum Points	Index Score
1 - Student Achievement	381	414	92
2 - Student Progress	440	800	55
3 - Closing Performance Gaps	350	400	88
4 - Postsecondary Readiness	N/A	N/A	N/A

System Safeguards

Number and Percent of Indicators Met

Performance Rates	12 out of 12 = 100%
Participation Rates	8 out of 8 = 100%
Graduation Rates	N/A
Total	**20 out of 20 = 100%**

	General Fund	%	Per Student	All Funds	%	Per Student
Expenditures by Object (Objects 6100-6600)						
Total Expenditures	3,141,135	100.00	7,972	3,455,872	100.00	8,771
Operating-Payroll	2,888,979	91.97	7,332	3,094,985	89.56	7,855
Other Operating	252,156	8.03	640	360,887	10.44	916
Non-Operating(Equipt/Supplies)	0	0.00	0	0	0.00	0
Expenditures by Function (Objects 6100-6400 Only)						
Total Operating Expenditures	3,141,135	100.00	7,972	3,455,872	100.00	8,771
Instruction (11,95) *	2,466,444	78.52	6,260	2,611,413	75.56	6,628
Instructional Res/Media (12) *	94,685	3.01	240	94,685	2.74	240
Curriculum/Staff Develop (13) *	53,352	1.70	135	53,497	1.55	136
Instructional Leadership (21) *	34,767	1.11	88	34,767	1.01	88
School Leadership (23) *	186,185	5.93	473	188,280	5.45	478
Guidance/Counseling Svcs (31) *	89,135	2.84	226	89,178	2.58	226
Social Work Services (32) *	7,476	0.24	19	7,476	0.22	19
Health Services (33) *	66,072	2.10	168	66,149	1.91	168
Food (35) **	0	0.00	0	166,639	4.82	423
Extracurricular (36) *	4	0.00	0	243	0.01	1
Plant Maint/Operation (51) * **	142,767	4.55	362	143,095	4.14	363
Security/Monitoring (52) * **	248	0.01	1	450	0.01	1
Data Processing Svcs (53)* **	0	0.00	0	0	0.00	0
Program expenditures by Program (Objects 6100-6400 only)						
Total Operating Expenditures	2,998,116	100.00	7,609	3,135,845	100.00	7,959
Regular	2,057,556	68.63	5,222	2,057,556	65.61	5,222
Gifted & Talented	42,841	1.43	109	42,841	1.37	109
Career & Technical	0	0.00	0	0	0.00	0
Students with Disabilities	703,460	23.46	1,785	841,189	26.82	2,135
Accelerated Education	81,328	2.71	206	81,328	2.59	206
Bilingual	112,931	3.77	287	112,931	3.60	287
Nondisc Alted-AEP Basic Serv	0	0.00	0	0	0.00	0
Disc Alted-DAEP Basic Serv	0	0.00	0	0	0.00	0
Disc Alted-DAEP Supplemental	0	0.00	0	0	0.00	0
T1 A Schoolwide-St Comp >=40%	0	0.00	0	0	0.00	0
Athletic Programming	0	0.00	0	0	0.00	0
High School Allotment	0	0.00	0	0	0.00	0

*

Note: Some amounts may not total due to rounding.

1/1

23

edutopia

WHAT WORKS IN EDUCATION
THE GEORGE LUCAS EDUCATIONAL FOUNDATION

TEACHER LEADERSHIP

What Parents Want in School Communication

AUGUST 31, 2011

Most of the population declares their New Year's resolutions January 1. For educators, it happens closer to September 1. And often high on the list: improving relationships with parents.

A new survey **(1)** from the National School Public Relations Association **(2)** (NSPRA) may be able to help you keep this one. Relationships are built on communication. And NSPRA recently surveyed 50 of its member districts (ranging from small to large and urban to rural, with a total of 43,310 responses in 22 states) to learn the communications preferences of both parents and non-parents.

The survey was quite informative as to how, and what, school districts should communicate with communities (many of NSPRA's members are district communications officials). But I think one of the most valuable uses for this survey will be in helping teachers and principals develop individual communications strategies for reaching out to parents.

How Parents Want School News

Consider, for example, that the survey asked parents their preferred delivery method for school news. Internet communications clearly won. The top five answers:

- E-mail from the district/school
- Online parent portal
- District/school e-newsletters
- District/school website
- Telephone/voice messaging system

As NSPRA President Ron Koehler points out, "Consumer needs are changing. The backpack folder is no longer the primary source of information for parents. They want and prefer instant electronic information. ... [T]he data demonstrates parents and non-parents alike turn to the web when they need information, and they want it now."

There is a twist, though: Social media (Facebook, Twitter and blogs) ranged near the **bottom** of communication preferences, below newspapers, television and attending school board meetings. More on

24

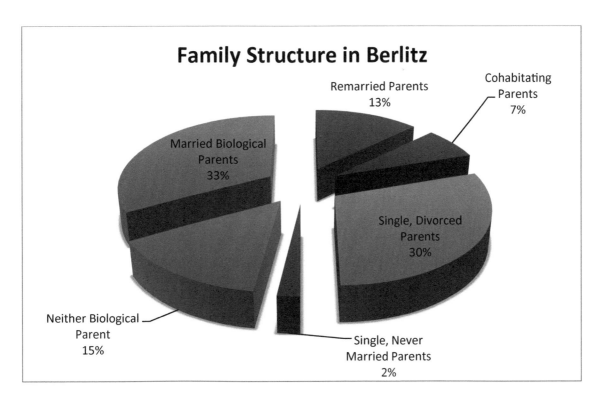

Family Structure in Berlitz

Remarried Parents
13%

Cohabitating Parents
7%

Married Biological Parents
33%

Single, Divorced Parents
30%

Neither Biological Parent
15%

Single, Never Married Parents
2%

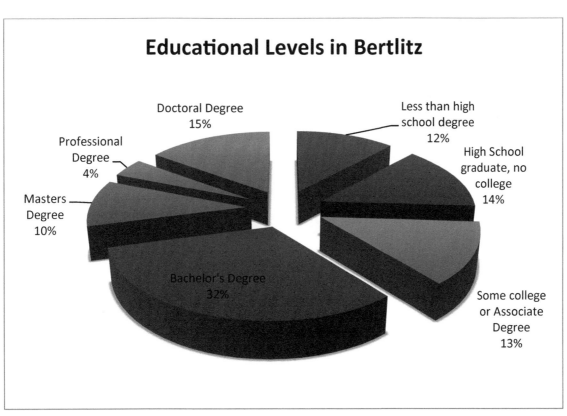

Educational Levels in Bertlitz

Doctoral Degree
15%

Professional Degree
4%

Masters Degree
10%

Bachelor's Degree
32%

Less than high school degree
12%

High School graduate, no college
14%

Some college or Associate Degree
13%

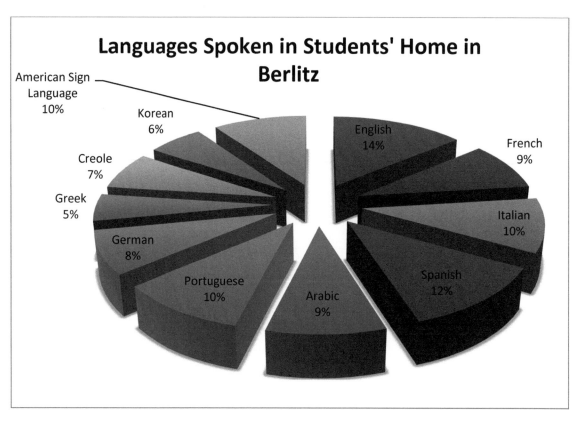

Languages Spoken in Students' Home in Berlitz

American Sign Language 10%
Korean 6%
Creole 7%
Greek 5%
German 8%
Portuguese 10%
Arabic 9%
Spanish 12%
Italian 10%
French 9%
English 14%

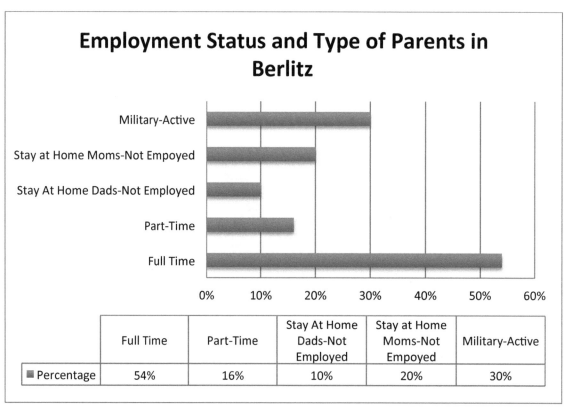

Employment Status and Type of Parents in Berlitz

	Full Time	Part-Time	Stay At Home Dads-Not Employed	Stay at Home Moms-Not Empoyed	Military-Active
■ Percentage	54%	16%	10%	20%	30%

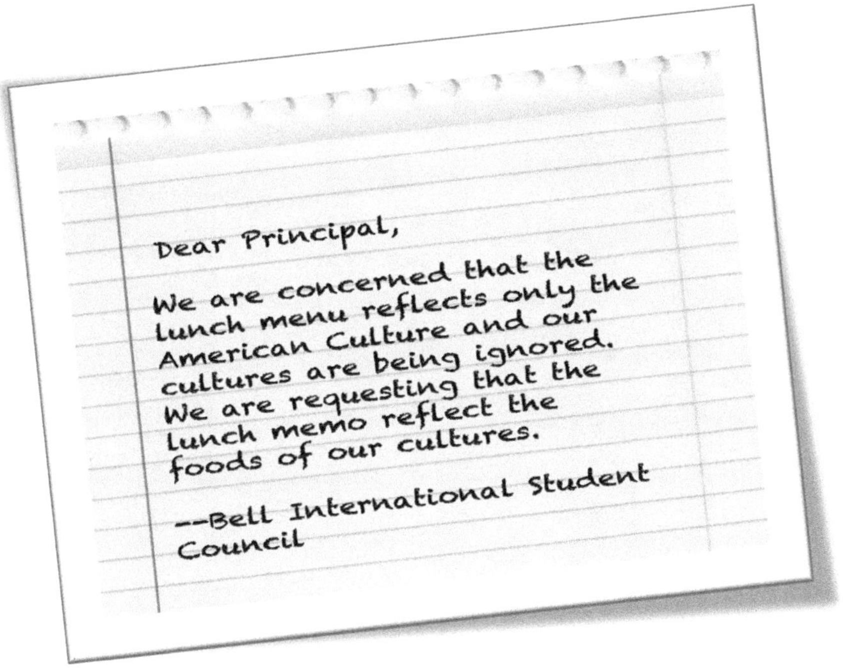

Dear Principal,

We are concerned that the
lunch menu reflects only the
American Culture and our
cultures are being ignored.
We are requesting that the
lunch memo reflect the
foods of our cultures.

--Bell International Student
Council

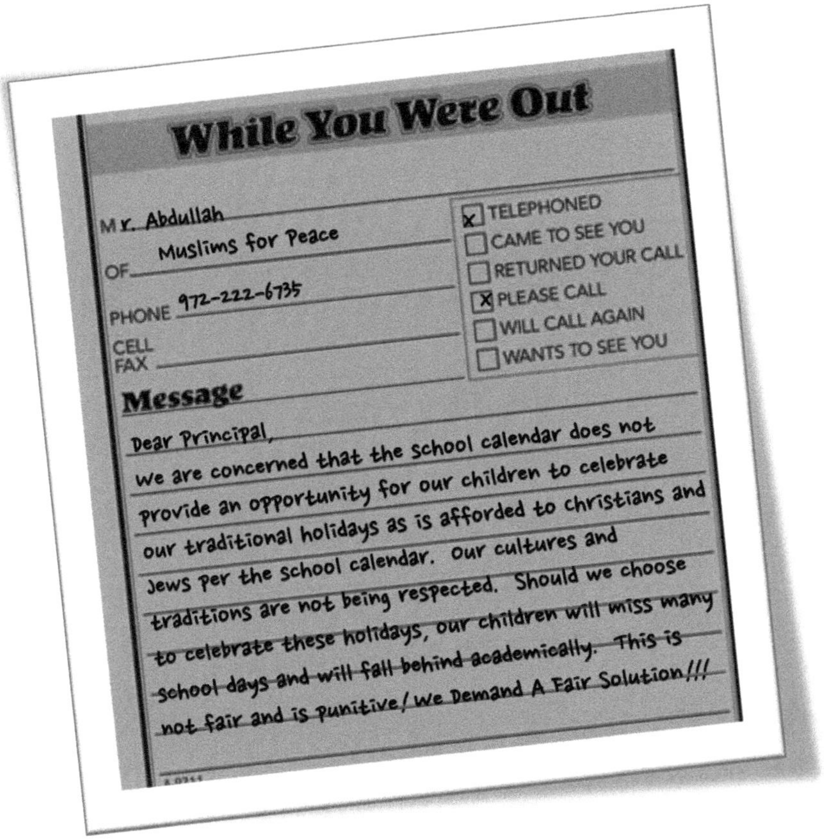

While You Were Out

Mr. Abdullah

OF Muslims for Peace

PHONE 972-222-6735

CELL

FAX

[x] TELEPHONED
[ ] CAME TO SEE YOU
[ ] RETURNED YOUR CALL
[x] PLEASE CALL
[ ] WILL CALL AGAIN
[ ] WANTS TO SEE YOU

Message

Dear Principal,

We are concerned that the School calendar does not
provide an opportunity for our children to celebrate
our traditional holidays as is afforded to Christians and
Jews per the School calendar. Our cultures and
traditions are not being respected. Should we choose
to celebrate these holidays, our children will miss many
school days and will fall behind academically. This is
not fair and is punitive! We Demand A Fair Solution!!!

Our parents are growing increasingly more concerned about the lack of information about how our students are performing academically and how the school budget is developed. There appears to be a great concern about the lack of money available to teachers to purchase supplies for special projects. We would would like for you to present the new accountability information and budget to our parents. Is there a way that you can send this information home to parents? We keep getting calls as well as PTA members being stopped on the street by parents wanting to know what's going on at the school. The parents seem not to be informed about special events, etc. At the last PTA meeting where the Principal presented information about the school, he only had documents in English and he did not have interpreters for the non Englishi Speaking parents. We have also have 8 paretns who are hearing impaired--they will need Sign Language Interpeters. I look forward to you attending our meeting--please have answers--our parents are threatening to take their issues to the school board.

PTA President

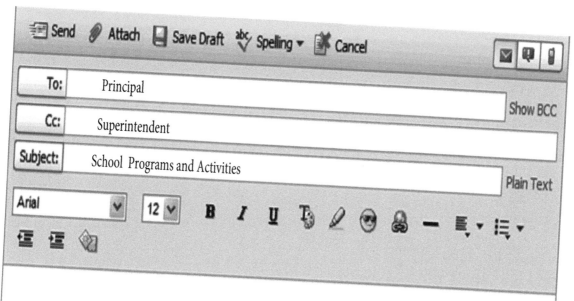

I just found the muli-cultural luncheon flyer in my son's book bag. The luncheon was last month and I would have liked to have participated--but I was not aware of this event. There must be a better way to communicate with parents other than sending the notices home in student book bags. Please rethink how you communicate with parents.

Mrs. Calbot
4th Grade Parent

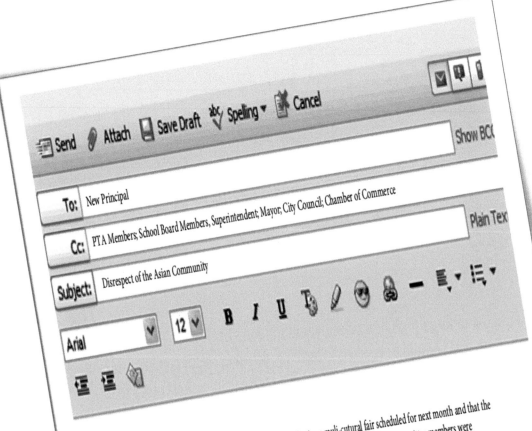

To: New Principal

Cc: PTA Members; School Board Members; Superintendent; Mayor; City Council; Chamber of Commerce

Subject: Disrespect of the Asian Community

The check out clerk at the Kroger informed me that our school was having a muli-cutural fair scheduled for next month and that the school was seeking donations. I would like to know if there was a committee formed and if so how committee members were selected and who those committee members are. Our community is diverse and all cultures should be represented. As a parent, PTA member and President of the Asian Cultural Society, I am offeneded that I was not made aware of this fair and further that I was not invited to assist with the planning of this event. What cultures will be represented in this fair? What organizations have committed to donating items and or services. Please contact me ASAP--this is very disheartening and disturubing. Please note that I will be bringing this issue before the School Board and to the City Council. I can only assume that since you did not contact the ONLY Asian organization is this community that you do not value and respect Asian Americans and this is UNACCEPTABLE.

SUPPLEMENTARY RESOURCES
CHAPTER THREE
COMPETENCY TWO

Books

Wilmore, E. L. (2013). *Passing the Special Education TExES Exam*. Corwin Press.

Texas Public School Organization and Administration: 2012
VORNBERG JAMES A (Author), CONSILIENCE LLC (Author), BORGEMENKE
ARTHUR J (

Auerbach, S. (2011). *School Leadership for Authentic Family and Community Partnerships: Research Perspectives for Transforming Practice*. Routledge, Taylor & Francis Group.

Visual Strategies for Improving Communication : Practical Supports for School & Home [Paperback]
Linda A. Hodgdon (Author)

School Communication that Works: A Patron-focused Approach to Delivering Your Message
Kenneth S. DeSieghardt (Author)

Why School Communication Matters: Strategies From PR Professionals [Paperback]
Kitty Porterfield (Author), Meg Carnes (Author)

Consensus-Oriented Decision-Making: The CODM Model for Facilitating Groups to Widespread Agreement Paperback. Tim Hartnett (Author)

Articles

Goldkind, L., & Farmer, G. (2013). The Enduring Influence of School Size and School Climate on Parents' Engagement in the School Community. *School Community Journal, 23*(1), 223-244.

Posey, L. (2012). Middle- and Upper-Middle-Class Parent Action for Urban Public Schools: Promise or Paradox?. *Teachers College Record, 114*(1),

Shatkin, G., & Gershberg, A. (2007). Empowering Parents and Building Communities: The Role of School-Based Councils in Educational Governance and Accountability. *Urban Education, 42*(6), 582-615.

Sprick, B., Rich, M., & Appleseed. (2010). *A Proposal to Strengthen Family and Community Engagement within the Elementary and Secondary Education Act: An Implementation Guide*. Appleseed.

Warren, M. R., Hong, S., Rubin, C., & Uy, P. (2009). Beyond the Bake Sale: A Community-Based Relational Approach to Parent Engagement in Schools. *Teachers College Record, 111*(9), 2209-2254.

Websites and Blogs

http://www.pta.org
http://www.txpta.org
http://www.pto.org
http://www.communityschools.org/scalingup/
http://communitypartnershipschool.org

Reports

What Parents Want in School Communication
http://www.edutopia.org/blog/parent-involvement-survey-anne-obrien

Effective Communication Between Parents and Teachers
http://theparentacademy.dadeschools.net/pdfs/Effective_Communication.pdf

Parent Communication Strategies
http://www.scholastic.com/teachers/collection/parent-communication-strategies

YouTube Videos

Ten Ways to Build School-Community Partnerships
Link
http://youtu.be/Lc_8Qjl2GPU-

Embed Code
<iframe width="560" height="315" src="//www.youtube.com/embed/Lc_8Qjl2GPU" frameborder="0" allowfullscreen></iframe>

Transforming Schools Through Family, School, and Community Engagement
Link
http://youtu.be/prMJgUM_CXI

Embed Code
<iframe width="560" height="315" src="//www.youtube.com/embed/prMJgUM_CXI" frameborder="0" allowfullscreen></iframe>

Mini Projects/Additional Assignments

1. Create a mock up of a school webpage that will allow two way school to family/community communication.
2. Create Newsletter
3. Assist PTA with parent engagement campaign to increase membership
4. Develop a comprehensive community relations campaign
5. Develop internal and external communications policy
6. Develop a plan for working effectively with the diverse school community to promote equal educational access for all students.

Discussion/Reflection Topics

To effectively communicate, we must realize that we are all different in the way we perceive the world and use this understanding as a guide to our communication with others.--*Tony Robbins*

Of all of our inventions for mass communication, pictures still speak the most universally understood language.--*Walt Disney*

"If two men on the same job agree all the time, then one is useless. If they disagree all the time, both are useless." - *Darryl F. Zanuck*

"If everyone is moving forward together, then success takes care of itself." - *Henry Ford*

Many ideas grow better when transplanted into another mind than the one where they sprang up." - *Oliver Wendell Holmes*

The strength of the team is each individual member. The strength of each member is the team." - *Phil Jackson*

Coming together is a beginning, staying together is progress, and working together is success." - *Henry Ford*

Collaboration isn't about being best friends, or even necessarily liking everyone you're working with. It *is* about putting all and any baggage aside, bringing your best self to the table, and focusing on the common goal--*Meghan M. Biro*

Truthful words are not beautiful; beautiful words are not truthful. Good words are not persuasive; persuasive words are not good.**Lao Tzu**

A man's character may be learned from the adjectives which he habitually uses in conversation. --*Mark Twain*
Any problem, big or small, within a family, always seems to start with bad communication. Someone isn't listening. *.Emma Thompson*

Electric communication will never be a substitute for the face of someone who with their soul encourages another person to be brave and true. --*Charles Dickens*

Effective communication is 20% what you know and 80% how you feel about what you know.--*Jim Rohn*

Chapter 4
TeXes Principal Competency 3

Justice Independent School District
124 Supreme Court Way
Litigation, TX 73030
903-736-3180
903-736-6739 (fax)
www.justiceisd.org

Dear New Principal,

Welcome to Justice Independent School District! We are extremely excited that you have accepted our offer to serve as the Principal of Thurgood Marshall Middle School of Humanity, Equity and Justice (TMMSHEJ). TMMSHEJ is the first school in the state of its kind. Students from all over the county have applied and been admitted to TMMSHEJ. Parents as well as students were particularly interested in and excited about TMMSHEJ because of the various programs, initiatives and academies that were established to support ALL students. We are most proud of our Gifted and Talented Academy, LGBT Academy, New Comers Academy, Single Gender Classes, Behavior Modification and Re-entry Program to name a few. Our students are exceptional and as such deserve to be educated in a school environment that recognizes, respects and supports their uniqueness. We have students who are new to the US and are non-English speaking, we have a cohort of students who are returning from a variety of juvenile justice facilities, students who have been classified as emotionally disturbed and students who qualify as members of MENSA to name just a few.

One of the key characteristics that we were looking for in the Principal for TMMSHEJ was an exceptional proven ability to act with integrity, fairness, and in an ethical and legal manner for all persons. Your commitment and advocacy for equitable access to a quality education for all students is what made you stand out from all of the other candidates. It will be essential that you continue to be an expert in the best practices impacting your exceptional student populations. The school community will look to you to inform them of new research, best practices and policies that will impact their children.

We would like to send out a press release—announcing your appointment as the new Principal. Please draft the announcement, you should discuss in some detail the uniqueness of the school to serve all students as well as your qualifications and commitment to serving successfully as the Principal of TMMSHEJ. The Press Release will be sent to a variety of news media outlets, parents, community members, students and elected officials. We are also excited about the possibility of our school earning the esteemed designation as a Middle School To Watch in Texas—we look forward to your presentation of this application to our school board in December. Once again, congratulations, we are so excited to have you as part of our team!

Educationally yours,

John "Jim Bo" Roberts

Superintendent
Justice Independent School District

Thurgood Marshall Middle School of Humanity, Equity and Justice

The Thurgood Marshall Middle School of Humanity, Equity and Justice, is an open enrollment middle school for all eligible county residents. TMMSHEJ has 410,000 square feet and was designed to hold 2,000 students. Its features include 45 academic classrooms, ten computer labs, six science labs, two library/media resource centers, full service school based clinic which includes a mental health division, a gymnasium, a six-lane pool, a dance studio/wrestling room, a 2,500-seat auditorium, a sports venue for track & field, football, soccer, rugby and lacrosse with bleacher space for 3,000 and classrooms devoted to the performing and visual arts.

Litigation, TX Demographics

Median Household income	$238,000
Percent of household earning >$200,000	65%
Percent of households earning < $10,0000	0%
Expenditures per student	$26,742
Percent local funding	90%

As the Principal of Thurgood Marshall, you will experience a variety challenges given the diversity and unique needs of your middle school student population. TMMSHEJ was built upon the tenets of the Middle School Philosophy that was so eloquently captured in the "This We Believe" report.

For this case, you will be presented with a variety of issues that will need to be resolved based on the TeXes Principal Competencies. Therefore, it is essential that you review all of the artifacts presented in this case study carefully. Identify the challenge and choose the best method for which you will address each concern. As you strategize to solve the challenges presented in this case, you will be expected to demonstrate a firm understanding and ability to do the following:

1. Model and promote the highest standard of conduct, ethical principles, and integrity in decision making, actions, and behaviors.

2. Implement policies and procedures that promote professional educator compliance with The Code of Ethics and Standard Practices for Texas Educators.

3. Apply knowledge of ethical issues affecting education.

4. Apply legal guidelines (e.g., in relation to students with disabilities, bilingual education, confidentiality, discrimination) to protect the rights of students and staff and to improve learning opportunities.

5. Apply laws, policies, and procedures in a fair and reasonable manner.

6. Articulate the importance of education in a free democratic society.

7. Serve as an advocate for all children.

8. Promote the continuous and appropriate development of all students.

9. Promote awareness of learning differences, multicultural awareness, gender sensitivity, and ethnic appreciation.

TEXAS EDUCATION AGENCY
Accountability Summary
Thurgood Marshall Middle

Accountability Rating

Met Standard

Met Standards on	Did Not Meet Standards on
- Student Achievement	- NONE
- Student Progress	
- Closing Performance Gaps	

Distinction Designation

Academic Achievement in Reading/ELA
Percent of Eligible Measures in Top Quartile 3 out of 4 = 75%
DISTINCTION EARNED

Academic Achievement in Mathematics
Percent of Eligible Measures in Top Quartile 3 out of 4 = 75%
DISTINCTION EARNED

Top 25 Percent Student Progress
NO DISTINCTION EARNED

Performance Index Report

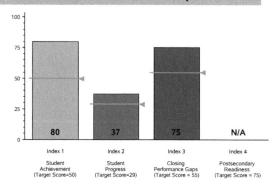

	Index 1	Index 2	Index 3	Index 4
	80	37	75	N/A
	Student Achievement (Target Score=50)	Student Progress (Target Score=29)	Closing Performance Gaps (Target Score = 55)	Postsecondary Readiness (Target Score = 75)

Campus Demographics

Campus Type	Middle School
Campus Size	1,749 Students
Grade Span	06 - 08
Percent Economically Disadvantaged	73.7%
Percent English Language Learners	11.0%
Mobility Rate	10.8%

Performance Index Summary

Index	Points Earned	Maximum Points	Index Score
1 - Student Achievement	3,944	4,936	80
2 - Student Progress	898	2,400	37
3 - Closing Performance Gaps	1,128	1,500	75
4 - Postsecondary Readiness	N/A	N/A	N/A

System Safeguards

Number and Percent of Indicators Met

Performance Rates	39 out of 39 = 100%
Participation Rates	18 out of 18 = 100%
Graduation Rates	N/A
Total	**57 out of 57 = 100%**

TEXAS EDUCATION AGENCY
Index 1: Student Achievement Data Table

STAAR Performance	All Students	African American	Hispanic	White	American Indian	Asian	Pacific Islander	Two or More Races	Special Ed	Econ Disadv	ELL
All Subjects											
Percent of Tests											
% at Phase-in 1 Level II or above	80%	72%	77%	89%	*	99%	*	78%	71%	75%	63%
% at Final Level II or above	40%	29%	32%	56%	*	90%	*	41%	39%	31%	15%
% at Level III Advanced	15%	7%	9%	27%	*	64%	*	17%	11%	9%	2%
Number of Tests											
# at Phase-in 1 Level II or above	3,944	909	1,509	1,357	*	82	*	79	507	2,695	327
# at Final Level II or above	1,969	365	629	859	*	75	*	41	281	1,119	76
# at Level III Advanced	761	93	185	413	*	53	*	17	81	330	8
Total Tests	4,936	1,269	1,950	1,521	*	83	*	101	713	3,598	518
Reading											
Percent of Tests											
% at Phase-in 1 Level II or above	82%	71%	80%	92%	*	96%	*	85%	71%	76%	62%
% at Final Level II or above	41%	31%	32%	60%	*	92%	*	53%	41%	32%	11%
% at Level III Advanced	18%	12%	10%	32%	*	65%	*	18%	14%	11%	1%
Number of Tests											
# at Phase-in 1 Level II or above	1,348	311	522	458	*	25	*	29	167	929	116
# at Final Level II or above	684	137	208	297	*	24	*	18	97	387	21
# at Level III Advanced	299	51	65	160	*	17	*	6	34	130	2
Total Tests	1,651	435	656	497	*	26	*	34	235	1,217	186
Mathematics											
Percent of Tests											
% at Phase-in 1 Level II or above	83%	72%	82%	92%	*	100%	*	78%	73%	78%	69%
% at Final Level II or above	43%	28%	38%	60%	*	93%	*	39%	38%	34%	15%
% at Level III Advanced	15%	4%	11%	26%	*	78%	*	19%	11%	9%	2%
Number of Tests											
# at Phase-in 1 Level II or above	1,363	313	536	457	*	27	*	28	173	947	127
# at Final Level II or above	709	121	251	298	*	25	*	14	89	407	28
# at Level III Advanced	250	19	73	130	*	21	*	7	25	106	4
Total Tests	1,649	433	654	496	*	27	*	36	236	1,214	185
Writing											
Percent of Tests											
% at Phase-in 1 Level II or above	74%	69%	73%	80%	-	100%	-	67%	63%	69%	51%
% at Final Level II or above	30%	21%	24%	42%	-	100%	-	40%	44%	24%	8%
% at Level III Advanced	5%	1%	3%	8%	-	25%	-	13%	7%	3%	4%
Number of Tests											
# at Phase-in 1 Level II or above	405	98	153	136	-	8	-	10	43	269	26
# at Final Level II or above	166	30	51	71	-	8	-	6	30	94	4
# at Level III Advanced	26	2	7	13	-	2	-	2	5	12	2
Total Tests	548	143	211	171	-	8	-	15	68	390	51

This indicator was not evaluated due to small numbers to protect student confidentiality.

TEXAS EDUCATION AGENCY
Index 1: Student Achievement Data Table

STAAR Performance	All Students	African American	Hispanic	White	American Indian	Asian	Pacific Islander	Two or More Races	Special Ed	Econ Disadv	ELL
Science											
Percent of Tests											
% at Phase-in 1 Level II or above	82%	79%	77%	92%	*	100%	*	75%	74%	78%	63%
% at Final Level II or above	44%	34%	32%	63%	*	91%	*	25%	43%	34%	25%
% at Level III Advanced	19%	7%	11%	34%	*	64%	*	13%	10%	12%	0%
Number of Tests											
# at Phase-in 1 Level II or above	448	102	165	163	*	11	*	6	64	304	30
# at Final Level II or above	237	44	68	113	*	10	*	2	37	133	12
# at Level III Advanced	101	9	24	60	*	7	*	1	9	45	0
Total Tests	544	129	215	178	*	11	*	8	87	389	48
Social Studies											
Percent of Tests											
% at Phase-in 1 Level II or above	70%	66%	62%	80%	*	100%	*	75%	69%	63%	58%
% at Final Level II or above	32%	26%	24%	45%	*	73%	*	13%	32%	25%	23%
% at Level III Advanced	16%	9%	7%	28%	*	55%	*	13%	9%	10%	0%
Number of Tests											
# at Phase-in 1 Level II or above	380	85	133	143	*	11	*	6	60	246	28
# at Final Level II or above	173	33	51	80	*	8	*	1	28	98	11
# at Level III Advanced	85	12	16	50	*	6	*	1	8	37	0
Total Tests	544	129	214	179	*	11	*	8	87	388	48

39

	General Fund	%	Per Student	All Funds	%	Per Student
Expenditures by Object (Objects 6100-6600)						
Total Expenditures	6,711,777	100.00	3,794	9,606,246	100.00	5,430
Operating-Payroll	6,380,800	95.07	3,607	8,624,083	89.78	4,875
Other Operating	330,977	4.93	187	944,209	9.83	534
Non-Operating(Equipt/Supplies)	0	0.00	0	37,954	0.40	21
Expenditures by Function (Objects 6100-6400 Only)						
Total Operating Expenditures	6,711,777	100.00	3,794	9,568,292	100.00	5,409
Instruction (11,95) *	4,844,085	72.17	2,738	6,930,257	72.43	3,918
Instructional Res/Media (12) *	150,241	2.24	85	150,241	1.57	85
Curriculum/Staff Develop (13) *	280,468	4.18	159	292,319	3.06	165
Instructional Leadership (21) *	264,174	3.94	149	316,772	3.31	179
School Leadership (23) *	615,604	9.17	348	621,010	6.49	351
Guidance/Counseling Svcs (31) *	388,282	5.79	219	389,268	4.07	220
Social Work Services (32) *	910	0.01	1	910	0.01	1
Health Services (33) *	120,022	1.79	68	120,022	1.25	68
Food (35) **	0	0.00	0	694,497	7.26	393
Extracurricular (36) *	47,991	0.72	27	52,436	0.55	30
Plant Maint/Operation (51) * **	0	0.00	0	560	0.01	0
Security/Monitoring (52) * **	0	0.00	0	0	0.00	0
Data Processing Svcs (53)* **	0	0.00	0	0	0.00	0
Program expenditures by Program (Objects 6100-6400 only)						
Total Operating Expenditures	6,663,786	100.00	3,767	8,820,799	100.00	4,986
Regular	4,822,847	72.37	2,726	6,306,411	71.49	3,565
Gifted & Talented	1,271	0.02	1	1,271	0.01	1
Career & Technical	695	0.01	0	695	0.01	0
Students with Disabilities	1,124,202	16.87	636	1,591,937	18.05	900
Accelerated Education	685,637	10.29	388	867,843	9.84	491
Bilingual	29,134	0.44	16	52,642	0.60	30
Nondisc Alted-AEP Basic Serv	0	0.00	0	0	0.00	0
Disc Alted-DAEP Basic Serv	0	0.00	0	0	0.00	0
Disc Alted-DAEP Supplemental	0	0.00	0	0	0.00	0
T1 A Schoolwide-St Comp >=40%	0	0.00	0	0	0.00	0
Athletic Programming	0	0.00	0	0	0.00	0
High School Allotment	0	0.00	0	0	0.00	0

*

Teacher Cultural Competence Survey Results

■ Agree   ■ Neutral   ■ Disagree

Statement	Agree	Neutral	Disagree
Encouraging pride in one's culture is the teachers' responsibility	15	55	30
Multiculural training for teachers is not necessary		95	05
In order to be an effective teacher, one needs to be aware of cultural differences present in the classroom	15	50	35
Students should learn to communicate in English only in my class		85	0 15
Teaching students about cultural diversity will only create conflict in my class		90	5 5
I actively offset language barriers that prevent communication in my class	0 15	85	
I actively challenge gender inequalities in my class	0 25	75	

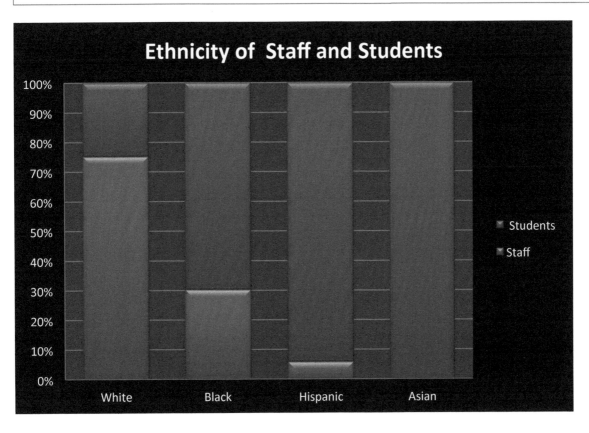

Ethnicity of Staff and Students

■ Students
■ Staff

White   Black   Hispanic   Asian

41

Dear Principal,

This is an ongoing issue. I've reported Ms. Janna's driving many times and nothing has been done about it. It's not just her driving. She does not like kids at all and she favors the white kids over the rest. She is mean to my daughters and does not care about their safety. She lets the big kids smoke and talk dirty on the bus. She throws away students' personal property if it's left on the bus. She does not wait for my kids to come out to catch the bus. I went out and tried to confront the bus driver once and she was very disrespectful and tried to drive away. She drives too fast and the bus tips going around curves. She does not give my kids time to sit down before she starts driving. When they get off the bus she is already in reverse and moving. She does not wait for them to get inside the house safely.

Mrs. J.K. Porkelly

Dear Principal

This teacher, Mr. Jones is constantly making racist comments towards his students. In his attempts to confront me about my grade in his class he said to work harder or I would end up like my ancestors, like "gardeners", just because I am Hispanic.

Guillerma R.

Dear Principal,

Ms. Temple, 8th grade Special Needs Teacher has proven herself incompetent on more than one occasion since the beginning of the school year. She has no respect for parents at all. She gives special education students work that is too hard or frustrating for them and then claims that they handle it just fine when the student tells the parent different. I want my child removed from this class immediatly!

Mrs. Dorothy James

Dear Principal

My teacher Ms. Score is a racist when we answer questions that are intelligent she ask us if we are really black. She also hits and grabs on students. 6 students filed a complaint against her and nothing happened. SOMETHING NEEDS TO HAPPEN! PLEASE HELP!

Send   Attach   Save Draft   Spelling   Cancel   Show BCC

To:	Principal	
		Plain Text
Cc:	Superintendent	
Subject:	Son Suspension	

Arial   12   **B** *I* U

My son is a LGBT youth who identifies as a female. My son wore makeup to school (eyeliner, eyeshadow, lipstick and blush). Your football coach made my son take the makeup off or be suspended. I believe that my son was discriminated against because he is transgender. Girls are permitted to wear makeup, why cant my son? I demand a written apology and the coach be FIRED! I have already contacted my attorney. My son feels so degraded he does not want to come back to school. We sent him to that school because of your LGBT program!!!!!!!!!!

Dear Principal

I am writing to you because I am gravely concerned that I seem to get the largest number of African American and Latino students assigned to me than any of my peers. It is not fair that I have to spend so much time correcting those students on their inappropriate behaviors and awful command of the English Language! They tend to be lazy and are not capable of performing simple tasks. We have other teachers who are African American and Latino, why cant they teach these children—I am sure that they can connect and understand them much better than I can. If you do not give me a better group of students, I will take a leave of absence from this school. I have already spoken with my doctor, and he agrees—working with low performing under achieving students is too much for me and is weakening my heart. I expect to hear from you about my new classroom and students within in the week.

Mr. Jones.

Dear Principal

We want to read Boy Meets Boy for our Spring Novel Assignment. Our teacher told us that the content of the book was inappropriate and that the book had no educational value. Here is the blurb from the book:

This is the story of Paul, a sophomore at a high school like no other: The cheerleaders ride Harleys, the homecoming queen used to be a guy named Daryl (she now prefers Infinite Darlene and is also the star quarterback), and the gay-straight alliance was formed to help the straight kids learn how to dance.

When Paul meets Noah, he thinks he's found the one his heart is made for. Until he blows it. The school bookie says the odds are 12-to-1 against him getting Noah back, but Paul's not giving up without playing his love really loud. His best friend Joni might be drifting away, his other best friend Tony might not be dealing with ultra-religious parents, and his ex-boyfriend Kyle might need it can really fit together right, but sometimes everything needs to fall apart before it can really fit together right.

This is a happy-meaningful romantic comedy about finding love, losing love, and doing what it takes to get love back in a crazy-wonderful world.

Other students are reading love stories for their Spring novel, this is not fair!!!!!

7th Grade LGBT Academy

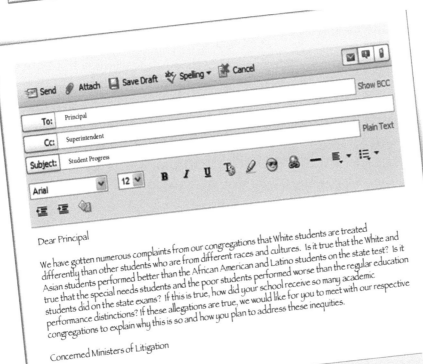

Dear Principal

We have gotten numerous complaints from our congregations that White students are treated differently than other students who are from different races and cultures. Is it true that the White and Asian students performed better than the African American and Latino students on the state test? Is it true that the special needs students and the poor students performed worse than the regular education students did on the state exams? If this is true, how did your school receive so many academic performance distinctions? If these allegations are true, we would like for you to meet with our respective congregations to explain why this is so and how you plan to address these inequities.

Concerned Ministers of Litigation

SUPPLEMENTARY RESOURCES
CHAPTER FOUR
COMPETENCY THREE

Books

Wilmore, E. L. (2013). *Passing the Special Education TExES Exam.* Corwin Press.

The Educator's Guide to Texas School Law: Seventh Edition [Paperback]
Jim Walsh (Author), Frank Kemerer (Author), Laurie Maniotis

Texas Public School Organization and Administration: 2012 [Misc. Supplies]
VORNBERG JAMES A (Author), CONSILIENCE LLC (Author), BORGEMENKE
ARTHUR J (Author)

Special Education Law by Laura F. Rothstein and Scott F. Johnson (Apr 17, 2013)

Bigham, G. (2013). Framework for Understanding the Legal Structure of Texas Public
Schools. *School Leadership*, 5.

Articles

Devine, D. (2013). Practising leadership in newly multi-ethnic schools: tensions in
the field?. *British Journal of sociology of education, 34*(3), 392-411.

Eddins, B., Russell, B., Farris, A., & Kirk, J. (2013, May). ETHICS TOOLS
ANCHORED BY ACTION LEARNING: A PRAXIS FRAMEWORK FOR
COLLABORATIVE DECISION MAKING. In *National Forum of Educational
Administration & Supervision Journal* (Vol. 30, No. 3).

Härtel, C. E., Butarbutar, I., Sendjaya, S., Pekerti, A., Hirst, G., & Ashkanasy, N.
M. (2013). Developing ethical leaders: a servant leadership approach.

Shapiro, J. P., & Gross, S. J. (2013). *Ethical educational leadership in turbulent
times:(Re) solving moral dilemmas.* Routledge.

Wilson, M. (2013). Critical reflection on authentic leadership and school leader
development from a virtue ethical perspective. *Educational Review*, (ahead-of-
print), 1-15.

Websites and Blogs

http://www.middlegradesforum.org
http://www.texasschoolstowatch.com
http://brandempowerment.com/schools/school-branding/
http://www.itgetsbetter.org
http://dreamact.info
www.tasb.org/
http://blogs.edweek.org/edweek/school_law/
http://www.nsba.org/schoollaw.aspx

Reports

Educators Code of Ethics
http://www.atpe.org/resources/atpenewsFall/10_news_fall_CodeofEthics.pdf
Growing up LGBT in America: HRC Youth Survey Report Key Findings

https://www.hrc.org/youth/about-the-survey-report#.Uv9P7vXnbFo

Evolved Thinking Putting Brands to Work to Advance Public School Education
http://edufundingpartners.com/FileUpload/pics/EFP%20White%20Paper%20-
%20Harnessing%20Brand%20Power%20to%20Advance%20Education%205-
12%20fin.pdf

Study Guide for This We Believe: Keys to Educating Young Adolescents
http://www.amle.org/portals/0/pdf/twb/TWB_StudyGuide_Aug2013.pdf

Helping Newcomer Students Succeed in Secondary Schools
http://www.cal.org/resources/pubs/helping-newcomer-students-succeed-in-secondary-
schools-and-beyond.html

How To Write A Policy Manual
http://www.templatezone.com/download-free-ebook/office-policy-manual-reference-
guide.pdf

YouTube Videos

Dr. Phil Has a Candid Discussion with LGBT Teens
http://youtu.be/A_vyMxGq1E0
EMBED CODE
<iframe width="420" height="315" src="//www.youtube.com/embed/A_vyMxGq1E0"
frameborder="0" allowfullscreen></iframe>

Oprah Winfrey: Teen Bullying LGBT & Straight Youths
http://youtu.be/LvMIOUuY11M
EMBED CODE

```
<iframe width="420" height="315" src="//www.youtube.com/embed/LvMIOUuY11M"
frameborder="0" allowfullscreen></iframe>
```

Dream Act only way for undocumented teens to serve
http://youtu.be/Qvwg0_BWk1A
EMBED CODE
```
<iframe width="560" height="315" src="//www.youtube.com/embed/Qvwg0_BWk1A"
frameborder="0" allowfullscreen></iframe>
```

Middle School Special Education Teacher Opens Her World Part 1
http://youtu.be/TBdufuPhEQ8
EMBED CODE
```
<iframe width="560" height="315" src="//www.youtube.com/embed/TBdufuPhEQ8"
frameborder="0" allowfullscreen></iframe>
```

Middle School Special Education Teacher Opens Her World Part 2
http://youtu.be/ybGfkr-GVZA
EMBED CODE
```
<iframe width="560" height="315" src="//www.youtube.com/embed/ybGfkr-GVZA"
frameborder="0" allowfullscreen></iframe>
```

Attorney and Parent Discuss Special Needs Trust and Related Concerns
http://youtu.be/wsiANOusGTg
EMBED CODE
```
<iframe width="560" height="315" src="//www.youtube.com/embed/wsiANOusGTg"
frameborder="0" allowfullscreen></iframe>
```

Mini Projects/Additional Assignments

1. Create PowerPoint Presentation to be presented to the school community outlining your first 100 days of school.
2. Create a 'BRANDING' Plan for your school.
3. Create year long staff development topics for your staff based on needs presented by the artifacts in this case.
4. Create PowerPoint Presentation to be presented to the school community on the DREAM Act.
5. Create PowerPoint Presentation for your staff on the findings from the Growing up LGBT in America: HRC Youth Survey Report Key Findings
6. Create a PowerPoint Presentation for your staff and community outlining your completed application for the School to Watch Initiative.
7. Create a logo to represent your school
8. Create a policy manual including forms delineating steps for resolving parent complaints.

9. Create a policy manual including forms delineating steps for resolving student complaints.
10. Create a policy manual including forms delineating steps for resolving teacher complaints.
11. Create a code of conduct policy including appropriate dress for staff and students.
12. Create a policy for student and teacher use of social media.

Discussion/Reflection Topics

1. Equality implies individuality. -Trey Anastasio

2. Until we get equality in education, we won't have an equal society. -Sonia Sotomayor

3. In America everybody is of opinion that he has no social superiors, since all men are equal, but he does not admit that he has no social inferiors, for, from the time of Jefferson onward, the doctrine that all men are equal applies only upwards, not downwards. ~Bertrand Russell, *Unpopular Essays*, 1950

4. We didn't all come over on the same ship, but we're all in the same boat. ~Bernard M. Baruch

5. It is well to know something of the manners of various peoples, in order more sanely to judge our own, and that we do not think that everything against our modes is ridiculous, and against reason, as those who have seen nothing are accustomed to think. ~René Descartes, *Discourse on the Method*, 1637 (translated)

6. All the people like us are We, And everyone else is They. ~Rudyard Kipling, *We and They*, 1926

7. The tears of the red, yellow, black, brown and white man are all the same. ~Martin H. Fischer

8. Equal distribution of wealth does not mean we all should be millionaires - it only means no one should die of hunger. ~Dodinsky, www.dodinsky.com

9. "Equality is not a concept. It's not something we should be striving for. It's a necessity. Equality is like gravity. We need it to stand on this earth as men and women, and the misogyny that is in every culture is not a true part of the human condition. It is life out of balance, and that imbalance is sucking something out of the soul of every man and woman who's confronted with it. We need equality. Kinda now." -- Joss Whedo

Chapter 5
TeXes Principal Competency 4

(Photo: By Brittany Carlson (USAG Stuttgart) (United States Army) [Public domain], via Wikimedia Commons)

Howard Gardner School for the Multiple Intelligences PTA

Dear New Principal,

Welcome to the Howard Gardner School for the Multiple Intelligences. We are very excited that you will be serving as our instructional leader. The members of the PTA membership are requesting that you offer a series of mini workshops for parents and other concerned community members to help us to better understand:

- The design and implementation of curricula and strategic plans that enhance teaching and learning;
- Alignment of curriculum, instruction, resources, and assessment;
- Varied assessments to measure student performance.

We are proud to have been awarded a School Improvement Grant of almost three million dollars to improve our school. It is important to us that our school is removed from the worst performing school list in Texas. Our membership is very much involved and engaged with all aspects of this school. We know that school/community-school to home communication and collaboration is necessary for student success. If we are to make informed decisions we must be knowledgeable about those issues that we are not expert in. This is where we will need your leadership. Parents must also understand the new state standards, the new curriculum and testing. We can support only that which we know and understand. We are looking for your leadership in understanding the trends in the education that can have both a negative and positive impact on the academic achievement of our children.

Once again, Welcome. I welcome the opportunity to work with you in strategizing in developing a workshop series for our parents. Our first PTA meeting will be in a month and I am requesting that you begin the first workshop of the series. I would like to send out an announcement and will need your input as to how many workshops will be facilitated and the content of each of the workshops.

In continued progress,

Jane Abrahams-Smith
President
PTA

THE HOWARD GARDNER SCHOOL FOR THE MULTIPLE INTELLIGENCES

Howard Gardner School for the Multiple Intelligences is located in Hammond, Texas The school is a few blocks south of Lake James, the Brown Horse Casino, and the Tams Marina. The Gardner School is surrounded by industry such as the B.K. Oil Refinery, Cargill, and Unilever.

The social-economic crunch has taken many jobs from parents in our district. Employment opportunities at local industries (BK Oil, steel mills, Unilever, Cargill) have dropped sharply in recent years. Minimum wage jobs like those recently created by the area's casino industry have not had enough positive economic impact to counteract the absence of previously mentioned jobs. Hopefully, many new investment announcements by Jenna Steel, BK Oil and the Horseshoe Casino should result in an economic upturn for the community.

For this case, you will be presented with a variety of challenges that will need to be resolved based on the TeXes Principal Competencies. Your PTA has high expectations and they are looking to you as their instructional leader to provide them with a "crash" course in the development, implementation and assessment of curricula. They are also interested in understanding current trends in education and how those trends may impact this school. Finally, they want assurances that the school will improve and be removed from the worst performing school list. Therefore, it is essential that you review all of the artifacts presented in this case study carefully. Each artifact should be viewed as an essential piece of the puzzle. To effectively address the needs of your school community you will need to put these essential pieces together to have an understanding of the challenges that are present in this school. Carefully identify each challenge and choose the best method for which you will address each concern. As you strategize to solve the challenges presented in this case, you will be expected to demonstrate a firm understanding and mastery of the following:

Facilitating effective campus curriculum planning based on knowledge of various factors (e.g., emerging issues, occupational and economic trends, demographic data, student learning data, motivation theory, teaching and learning theory, principles of curriculum design, human developmental processes, legal requirements).

Facilitating the use of sound, research-based practice in the development, implementation, and evaluation of campus curricular, co-curricular, and extracurricular programs.

Facilitating campus participation in collaborative district planning, implementation, monitoring, and revision of curriculum to ensure appropriate scope, sequence, content, and alignment.

Facilitating the use of appropriate assessments to measure student learning and ensure educational accountability.

Facilitating the use of technology, telecommunications, and information systems to enrich the campus curriculum.

Facilitating the effective coordination of campus curricular, co-curricular, and extracurricular programs in relation to other district programs.

Promoting the use of creative thinking, critical thinking, and problem solving by staff and other campus stakeholders involved in curriculum design and delivery.

TEXAS EDUCATION AGENCY
2013 Accountability Summary

Accountability Rating

Improvement Required

Met Standards on	Did Not Meet Standards on
- Student Achievement	- Closing Performance Gaps
- Student Progress	

Distinction Designation

Academic Achievement in Reading/ELA

Percent of Eligible Measures in Top Quartile
2 out of 4 = 50%

DOES NOT QUALIFY

Academic Achievement in Mathematics

Percent of Eligible Measures in Top Quartile
1 out of 3 = 33%

DOES NOT QUALIFY

Top 25 Percent Student Progress

DOES NOT QUALIFY

Performance Index Report

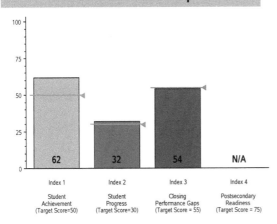

	Index 1	Index 2	Index 3	Index 4
Score	62	32	54	N/A
	Student Achievement (Target Score=50)	Student Progress (Target Score=30)	Closing Performance Gaps (Target Score = 55)	Postsecondary Readiness (Target Score = 75)

Campus Demographics

Campus Type	Elementary
Campus Size	658 Students
Grade Span	KG - 05
Percent Economically Disadvantaged	88.4%
Percent English Language Learners	36.5%
Mobility Rate	26.6%

Performance Index Summary

Index	Points Earned	Maximum Points	Index Score
1 - Student Achievement	400	650	62
2 - Student Progress	379	1,200	32
3 - Closing Performance Gaps	431	800	54
4 - Postsecondary Readiness	N/A	N/A	N/A

System Safeguards

Number and Percent of Indicators Met

Performance Rates	13 out of 18 = 72%
Participation Rates	12 out of 12 = 100%
Graduation Rates	N/A
Total	**25 out of 30 = 83%**

TEXAS EDUCATION AGENCY
2013 Index 3: Closing Performance Gaps Calculation Report

Overall Performance

STAAR Weighted Performance Rate	Econ Disadv	African American	White	Total Points	Maximum Points
Reading Weighted Performance	64	60	0	124	200
Mathematics Weighted Performance	56	48	0	104	200
Writing Weighted Performance	47	40	0	87	200
Science Weighted Performance	60	56	0	116	200
Social Studies Weighted Performance	0	0	0	0	0
Total				431	800
Index 3 Score					**54**

Note: For 2013, Weighted Performance Rate is equal to the percent of tests that meet Phase-in 1 Level II or above.

Reading Performance

STAAR Weighted Performance Rate	Econ Disadv	African American	White	Total Points	Maximum Points
Number of Tests	165	108			
# at Phase-in 1 Level II or above	106	65			
% at Phase-in 1 Level II or above	64	60			
Reading Weighted Performance Rate	**64**	**60**	**0**	**124**	**200**

Mathematics Performance

STAAR Weighted Performance Rate	Econ Disadv	African American	White	Total Points	Maximum Points
Number of Tests	166	108			
# at Phase-in 1 Level II or above	93	52			
% at Phase-in 1 Level II or above	56	48			
Mathematics Weighted Performance Rate	**56**	**48**	**0**	**104**	**200**

TEXAS EDUCATION AGENCY
2013 Index 3: Closing Performance Gaps Data Table

	African American	Hispanic	White	American Indian	Asian	Pacific Islander	Two or More Races	Econ Disadv
2012 STAAR Performance								
All Subjects - Used for Determining Lowest Performing Race/Ethnicity Group(s)								
Percent of Tests								
% at Phase-in 1 Level II or above	62%	74%	72%	*	71%	-	**	
Number of Tests								
Total Tests	301	283	53	*	17	-	**	
2013 STAAR Performance								
Reading								
Percent of Tests								
% at Phase-in 1 Level II or above	60%	75%	74%	*	*	-	*	64%
% at Final Level II or above	20%	43%	16%	*	*	-	*	24%
% at Level III Advanced	9%	15%	11%	*	*	-	*	10%
Number of Tests								
# at Phase-in 1 Level II or above	65	40	14	*	*	-	*	106
# at Final Level II or above	22	23	3	*	*	-	*	39
# at Level III Advanced	10	8	2	*	*	-	*	17
Total Tests	108	53	19	*	*	-	*	165
Mathematics								
Percent of Tests								
% at Phase-in 1 Level II or above	48%	65%	63%	*	*	-	*	56%
% at Final Level II or above	15%	22%	26%	*	*	-	*	17%
% at Level III Advanced	1%	11%	5%	*	*	-	*	4%
Number of Tests								
# at Phase-in 1 Level II or above	52	35	12	*	*	-	*	93
# at Final Level II or above	16	12	5	*	*	-	*	28
# at Level III Advanced	1	6	1	*	*	-	*	6
Total Tests	108	54	19	*	*	-	*	166

	General Fund	%	Per Student	All Funds	%	Per Student
Expenditures by Object (Objects 6100-6600)						
Total Expenditures	3,629,961	100.00	4,993	4,056,525	100.00	5,580
Operating-Payroll	3,362,873	92.64	4,626	3,572,620	88.07	4,914
Other Operating	265,477	7.31	365	482,294	11.89	663
Non-Operating(Equipt/Supplies)	1,611	0.04	2	1,611	0.04	2
Expenditures by Function (Objects 6100-6400 Only)						
Total Operating Expenditures	3,628,350	100.00	4,991	4,054,914	100.00	5,578
Instruction (11,95) *	2,629,470	72.47	3,617	2,817,639	69.49	3,876
Instructional Res/Media (12) *	92,985	2.56	128	95,029	2.34	131
Curriculum/Staff Develop (13) *	100,668	2.77	138	103,293	2.55	142
Instructional Leadership (21) *	59,096	1.63	81	59,096	1.46	81
School Leadership (23) *	260,240	7.17	358	260,732	6.43	359
Guidance/Counseling Svcs (31) *	156,503	4.31	215	156,503	3.86	215
Social Work Services (32) *	10,678	0.29	15	10,678	0.26	15
Health Services (33) *	72,294	1.99	99	72,294	1.78	99
Food (35) **	0	0.00	0	221,538	5.46	305
Extracurricular (36) *	880	0.02	1	8,775	0.22	12
Plant Maint/Operation (51) * **	237,059	6.53	326	240,860	5.94	331
Security/Monitoring (52) * **	8,477	0.23	12	8,477	0.21	12
Data Processing Svcs (53)* **	0	0.00	0	0	0.00	0
Program expenditures by Program (Objects 6100-6400 only)						
Total Operating Expenditures	3,265,716	100.00	4,492	3,388,593	100.00	4,661
Regular	2,090,945	64.03	2,876	2,099,808	61.97	2,888
Gifted & Talented	0	0.00	0	0	0.00	0
Career & Technical	0	0.00	0	0	0.00	0
Students with Disabilities	586,557	17.96	807	608,198	17.95	837
Accelerated Education	139,906	4.28	192	232,279	6.85	320
Bilingual	448,308	13.73	617	448,308	13.23	617
Nondisc Alted-AEP Basic Serv	0	0.00	0	0	0.00	0
Disc Alted-DAEP Basic Serv	0	0.00	0	0	0.00	0
Disc Alted-DAEP Supplemental	0	0.00	0	0	0.00	0
T1 A Schoolwide-St Comp >=40%	0	0.00	0	0	0.00	0
Athletic Programming	0	0.00	0	0	0.00	0
High School Allotment	0	0.00	0	0	0.00	0

Texas Campus STaR Chart Summary
1 = Early Tech 2 = Developing Tech 3 = Advanced Tech 4 = Target Tech

Key Area I: Teaching and Learning

TL1	TL2	TL3	TL4	TL5	TL6	Total
Patterns of Classroom Use	Frequency/ Design of Instructional Setting	Content Area Connections	Techology Applications (TA) TEKS Implemention	Student Mastery of Technology Applications	Online Learning	Total
1	1	2	2	2	1	9

Key Area II: Educator Preparation and Development

EP1	EP2	EP3	EP4	EP5	EP6	Total
Professional Development Experiences	Models of Professional Development	Capabilities of Educators	Access to Professional Development	Levels of Understanding and Patterns of Use	Professional Development for Online Learning	Total
2	2	2	2	2	2	12

Key Area III: Leadership, Administration and Instructional Support

L1	L2	L3	L4	L5	L6	Total
Leadership and Vision	Planning	Instructional Support	Communication and Collaboration	Budget	Leadership and Support for Online Learning	Total
2	2	2	2	2	2	12

Key Area IV: Infrastructure for Technology

INF1	INF2	INF3	INF4	INF5	INF6	Total
Students per Computers	Internet Access Connectivity Speed	Other Classroom Technology	Technical Support	Local Area Network Wide Area Network	Distance Learning Capacity	Total
1	2	1	1	2	2	9

KEY AREA SUMMARY

Key Area	Key Area Total	Key Area STaR Classification
I. Teaching and Learning	9	EarlyTech
II. Educator Preparation and Development	12	Developing Tech
III. LeaderShip, Admin., Instructional Support	12	Developing Tech
IV. Infrastructure for Technology	9	Early Tech

58

September 28, 2014

Dear Principal,

I am pleased to provide the enclosed grant award notification (GAN) for the Race to the Top Assessment program, as funded by the American Recovery and Reinvestment Act (ARRA). These funds are being awarded on the basis of the approved budget of $2,990,272 for the School Improvement Grant (SIG) for the Howard Gardner School for the Multiple Intelligences.

Congratulations to you and others participating in SIG on your hard work and accomplishment. As the Secretary noted in his remarks on September 2nd when he announced the Race to the Top Assessment winners, if America is to have a public school system second to none, each state needs a first-rate assessment system to measure progress, guide instruction, and prepare students for college and careers. This is important and challenging work. I look forward to working with SIG in support of your efforts to develop the next generation of assessment systems on behalf of educators, students and families across the country.

This award is subject to the attached grant conditions related to administering the grant, monitoring sub-recipients, reporting, maintaining adequate financial controls and procedures regarding the selection, award, and administration of contracts or agreements. Further, in accordance with 34 CFR 75.234(b), this award is classified as a cooperative agreement and will include substantial involvement on the part of the Department of Education (Department) program contact. As noted in the grant award documents, we expect that SIG and the Department will successfully negotiate and complete a final cooperative agreement the recipient signs and returns no later than January 7.

In addition, I am enclosing a second GAN for a supplemental award of $872,697. These funds support efforts to help participating schools successfully transition to innovative curriculum and assessments. As soon as possible but no later than January 7, or when the cooperative agreement is signed (if sooner), the consortium will complete a plan that details transition strategies and activities recommended to the Department by the peer reviewers. The final approved plan and budget for this supplemental award will be incorporated into the cooperative agreement that is signed by the consortium and the Department.

www.ed.gov

400 MARYLAND AVE., SW, WASHINGTON, DC 20202-6200

The Department of Education's mission is to promote student achievement and preparation for global competitiveness by fostering educational excellence and ensuring equal access.

59

Grade Level Breakdown of Student Multiple Intelligences
Kindergarten

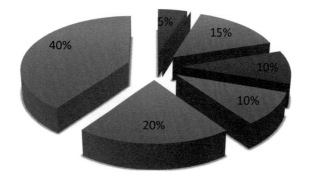

- Nature Smart (Naturalist)
- People Smart (Interpersonal)
- Number Smart (Logical)
- Picture Smart (Spatial Visual)
- Self Smart (Intrapesonal)
- Body Smart (Kinesthetic)
- Music Smart (Musical)
- Word Smart (Linguistic)

Grade Level Breakdown of Student Multiple Intelligences
First Grade

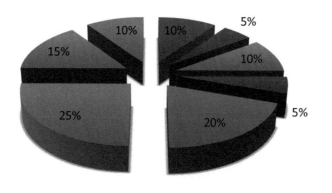

- Nature Smart (Naturalist)
- People Smart (Interpersonal)
- Number Smart (Logical)
- Picture Smart (Spatial Visual)
- Self Smart (Intrapesonal)
- Body Smart (Kinesthetic)
- Music Smart (Musical)
- Word Smart (Linguistic)

Grade Level Breakdown of Student Multiple Intelligences
Second Grade

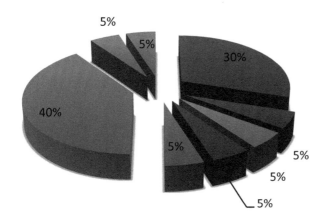

- ■ Nature Smart (Naturalist)
- ■ People Smart (Interpersonal)
- ■ Number Smart (Logical)
- ■ Picture Smart (Spatial Visual)
- ■ Self Smart (Intrapesonal)
- ■ Body Smart (Kinesthetic)
- ■ Music Smart (Musical)
- ■ Word Smart (Linguistic)

Grade Level Breakdown of Student Multiple Intelligences
Third Grade

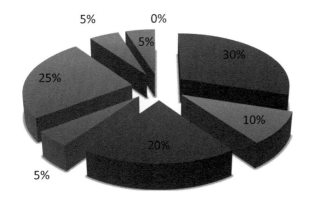

- ■ Nature Smart (Naturalist)
- ■ People Smart (Interpersonal)
- ■ Number Smart (Logical)
- ■ Picture Smart (Spatial Visual)
- ■ Self Smart (Intrapesonal)
- ■ Body Smart (Kinesthetic)
- ■ Music Smart (Musical)
- ■ Word Smart (Linguistic)

Grade Level Breakdown of Student Multiple Intelligences
Fourth Grade

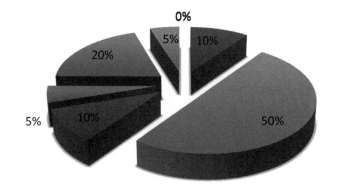

- Nature Smart (Naturalist)
- People Smart (Interpersonal)
- Number Smart (Logical)
- Picture Smart (Spatial Visual)
- Self Smart (Intrapesonal)
- Body Smart (Kinesthetic)
- Music Smart (Musical)
- Word Smart (Linguistic)

Grade Level Breakdown of Student Multiple Intelligences
Fifth Grade

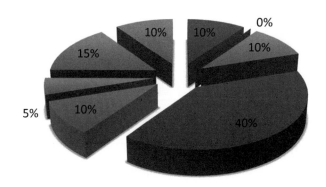

- Nature Smart (Naturalist)
- People Smart (Interpersonal)
- Number Smart (Logical)
- Picture Smart (Spatial Visual)
- Self Smart (Intrapesonal)
- Body Smart (Kinesthetic)
- Music Smart (Musical)
- Word Smart (Linguistic)

Co-Curricular Assignments by Grade Level	
Activity	**Grade Level**
Music	2,3,4
Dance	2,3,5
Gymnastics	K,4,5
Reading Club	K,1,2,3,4,5
Choir	3,4
Art	1,2
Robotics	1,2,5
Chess	1,2,3
Debate	3,4
Garden Club	K,3,4

External Auditor Report on Curriculum

Characteristics:	Auditors' Rating	
	Adequate	Inadequate
1. Describes the philosophical framework for the design of the curriculum, including such directives as standards-based, results-based, or competency-based; the alignment of the written, taught, and tested curriculum; and the approaches used in delivering the curriculum.		X
2. Identifies the timing, scope, and procedures for a periodic cycle of review of curriculum in all subject areas and at all grade levels.		X
3. Defines and directs the stages of curriculum development.		X
4. Specifies the roles and responsibilities of the board, central office staff members, and school-based staff members in the design and delivery of curriculum.		X
5. Presents the format and components of all curriculum, assessments, and instructional guide documents.		X
6. Directs how state and national standards will be considered in the curriculum. This includes whether or not to use a backloaded approach, in which the curriculum is derived from high-stakes tested learnings (topological and/or deep alignment), and/ or a frontloaded approach, which derives the curriculum from national, state, or local learnings.		X
7. Requires for every content area a focused set of precise student objectives/student expectations and standards that are reasonable in number so the student has adequate time to master the content.		X
8. Directs that curriculum documents not only specify the content of the student objectives/student expectations, but also include multiple contexts and cognitive types.		X
9. Specifies the overall beliefs and procedures governing the assessment of curriculum effectiveness. This includes curriculum-based diagnostic assessments and rubrics (as needed). Such assessments direct instructional decisions regarding student progress in mastering prerequisite concepts, skills, knowledge, and long-term mastery of the learning.		X
10. Directs curriculum to be designed so that it supports teachers' differentiation of instructional approaches and selection of student objectives at the right level of difficulty. This ensures that those students who need prerequisite concepts, knowledge, and skills are moved ahead at an accelerated pace, and that students who have already mastered the objectives are also moved ahead at a challenging pace.		X
11. Describes the procedures teachers and administrators will follow in using assessment data to strengthen written curriculum and instructional decision making.		X
12. Outlines procedures for conducting formative and summative evaluations of programs and their corresponding curriculum content.		X
13. Requires the design of a comprehensive staff development program linked to curriculum design and its delivery.		X
14. Presents procedures for monitoring the delivery of curriculum.		X
15. Establishes a communication plan for the process of curriculum design and delivery.		X
Total	**0**	**15**
Percentage of Adequacy	**0%**	

External Auditors' Assessment of Staff Development Program

Characteristics	Adequate	Inadequate
Policy		
1. Has policy that directs staff development efforts.		X
2. Fosters an expectation for professional growth.	X	
3. Is for all employees.	X	
Planning and Design		
4. Is based on a careful analysis of data and is data-driven.		X
5. Provides for system-wide coordination and has a clearinghouse function in place.		X
6. Provides the necessary funding to carry out professional development goals.	X	
7. Has a current plan that provides a framework for integrating innovations related to mission.		X
8. Has a professional development mission in place.	X	
9. Is built using a long-range planning approach.		X
10. Provides for organizational, unit, and individual development in a systemic manner.		X
11. Focuses on organizational change—staff development efforts are aligned to district goals.		X
Delivery		
12. Is based on proven research-based approaches that have been shown to increase productivity.		X
13. Provides for three phases of the change process: initiation, implementation, and institutionalization.		X
14. Is based on human learning and development and adult learning		X
15. Uses a variety of professional development approaches.	X	
16. Provides for follow-up and on-the-job application necessary to ensure improvement.		X
17. Expects each supervisor to be a staff developer of staff supervised.		X
Evaluation		
18. Requires an evaluation process that is ongoing, includes multiple sources of information, focuses on all levels of the organization, and is based on actual change in behavior.		X
Total	5	13
Percentage	28%	

SUPPLEMENTARY RESOURCES
CHAPTER FIVE
COMPETENCY FOUR

Books

Wilmore, E. L. (2013). *Passing the Special Education TExES Exam.* Corwin Press.

Texas Public School Organization and Administration: 2012 [Misc. Supplies] VORNBERG JAMES A (Author), CONSILIENCE LLC (Author), BORGEMENKE ARTHUR J (Author)

SuperVision and Instructional Leadership: A Developmental Approach (9th Edition) (Allyn & Bacon Educational Leadership... by Glickman, Carl D., Gordon, Stephen P. and Ross-Gordon, Jovita M. (Jan 24, 2013)

Instructional Coaches and the Instructional Leadership Team: A Guide for School-Building Improvement by Spaulding, Dean T. and Smith, Gail M. (Aug 8, 2012)

Leverage Leadership: A Practical Guide to Building Exceptional Schools by Bambrick-Santoyo, Paul, Lemov, Doug and Peiser, Brett (Jun 7, 2012)

Planning in the Face of Conflict: The Surprising Possibilities of Facilitative Leadership by John F. Forester (Sep 6, 2013)

Smart Leaders, Smarter Teams: How You and Your Team Get Unstuck to Get Results by Schwarz, Roger M. (Feb 26, 2013)

Multicultural Partnerships: Involve All Families by Hutchins, Darcy, Epstein, Joyce and Greenfeld, Marsha (Sep 27, 2013)

Articles

Squires, D. (2012). Curriculum alignment research suggests that alignment can improve student achievement. *The Clearing House: A Journal of Educational Strategies, Issues and Ideas, 85*(4), 129-135.

Raska, D., Heights, H., Keller, E. W., & Shaw, D. (2012). CURRICULUM ALIGNMENT FOR IMPROVED LEARNING OUTCOMES. *Marketing Theory and Applications*, 318.

Dill, L. J. (2013). *A comparative study between CSCOPE and non-CSCOPE districts and corresponding effect of curriculum on English language learners* (Doctoral dissertation, TEXAS A&M UNIVERSITY-COMMERCE).

Porter, A., McMaken, J., Hwang, J., & Yang, R. (2011). Common core standards the new US intended curriculum. *Educational Researcher, 40*(3), 103-116.

Porter, A., McMaken, J., Hwang, J., & Yang, R. (2011). Assessing the Common Core Standards Opportunities for Improving Measures of Instruction. *Educational researcher, 40*(4), 186-188.

Robinson, V. M. (2010). From instructional leadership to leadership capabilities: Empirical findings and methodological challenges. *Leadership and Policy in Schools, 9*(1), 1-26.

Horng, E., & Loeb, S. (2010). New thinking about instructional leadership. *Phi Delta Kappan, 92*(3), 66-69.

Neumerski, C. M. (2013). Rethinking Instructional Leadership, a Review What Do We Know About Principal, Teacher, and Coach Instructional Leadership, and Where Should We Go From Here?. *Educational administration quarterly, 49*(2), 310-347.

Mendels, P. (2012). The effective principal. *JDS: The learning forward journal, 33*(1).

Websites and Blogs

http://www.tea.state.tx.us
http://www.corestandards.org
http://pdkintl.org/publications/kappan/
http://www.edweek.org/ew/index.html
http://www.naesp.org
http://learningforward.org/publications/learning-principal#.UxpZXxbog4M
http://www.wallacefoundation.org/Pages/default.aspx

Reports

Confrey, J., & Krupa, E. (2010). Curriculum Design, Development, and Implementation in an Era of Common Core State Standards. Summary Report of a Conference (Arlington, Virginia, August 1-3, 2010). *Center for the Study of Mathematics Curriculum*.

Hallinger, P. (2011). A review of three decades of doctoral studies using the Principal Instructional Management Rating Scale: A lens on methodological progress in educational leadership. *Educational Administration Quarterly, 47*(2), 271-306.

YouTube Videos

Common Core Curriculum - A Trojan Horse for Education Re
Link
http://youtu.be/hxYfimNeCtY
Embed Code
<iframe width="560" height="315" src="//www.youtube.com/embed/hxYfimNeCtY" frameborder="0" allowfullscreen></iframe>

Kelly Shackelford explaining the new social studies curriculum in Texas
Link
http://youtu.be/RDRT4J55ePc

Embed Code
<iframe width="560" height="315" src="//www.youtube.com/embed/RDRT4J55ePc" frameborder="0" allowfullscreen></iframe>

Anderson Cooper 360° : Texas textbook changes
Link
http://youtu.be/ad3rytLNk3k

Embed Code
<iframe width="560" height="315" src="//www.youtube.com/embed/ad3rytLNk3k" frameborder="0" allowfullscreen></iframe>

Connecting the Dots ~ Common Core Curriculum with Texas's CSCOPE
Link
http://youtu.be/zLkmjQM89H0

Embed Code
<iframe width="560" height="315" src="//www.youtube.com/embed/zLkmjQM89H0" frameborder="0" allowfullscreen></iframe>

Common Core Standards - Fact and Fiction
Link
http://youtu.be/EXf91AGW2QA

Embed Code
<iframe width="420" height="315" src="//www.youtube.com/embed/EXf91AGW2QA" frameborder="0" allowfullscreen></iframe>

Dr. Joyce Epstein on schools and families
Link
http://youtu.be/z1T_5qVy1gU

Embed
<iframe width="560" height="315" src="//www.youtube.com/embed/z1T_5qVy1gU" frameborder="0" allowfullscreen></iframe>

Principles of teaching - partnership with parents
Link
http://www.youtube.com/watch?v=FRwMUnCjVrc&list=PLvzOwE5lWqhRPzheyprYHc
A8SZl9Qvnpz&feature=share&index=5

Embed Code
<iframe width="560" height="315"
src="//www.youtube.com/embed/FRwMUnCjVrc?list=PLvzOwE5lWqhRPzheyprYHcA
8SZl9Qvnpz" frameborder="0" allowfullscreen></iframe>

Mini Projects/Additional Assignments

Create a curriculum area of your school webpage where you will delineate how you plan to facilitate effective campus curriculum planning based on knowledge of various factors (e.g., emerging issues, occupational and economic trends, demographic data, student learning data, motivation theory, teaching and learning theory, principles of curriculum design, human developmental processes, legal requirements).

You have an opportunity to apply for $150 grant for the implementation and alignment of a curriculum that will help improve student academic achievement. Create a presentation that you will present to the funders of this grant as to how you will facilitate the use of sound, research-based practice in the development, implementation, and evaluation of campus curricular, co-curricular, and extracurricular programs.

Develop staff development activities that will help you to facilitate campus participation in collaborative district planning, implementation, monitoring, and revision of curriculum to ensure appropriate scope, sequence, content, and alignment.

Create a PowerPoint Present where you share your plan for the use of appropriate assessments to measure student learning and ensure educational accountability. The PowerPoint will be presented to your staff during the first day back at school

Create plan to facilitate the use of technology, telecommunications, and information systems to enrich the campus curriculum. This plan will be presented to your school board.

Create plan for facilitating the effective coordination of campus curricular, co-curricular, and extracurricular programs in relation to other district programs. The plan would be presented to the PTA, teachers, students and coaches.

Create a presentation and PR Plan where you demonstrate how you intend to promote the use of creative thinking, critical thinking, and problem solving by staff and other campus stakeholders involved in curriculum design and delivery. This plan will be presented to the School Board.

Discussion/Reflection Topics

1. 'Could it be that the current education reforms have not yet fully dealt with what teaching and learning are all about? In a word, yes.' Peyton Williams ASCD President 2003

2. 'Standardization, the great ally of mediocrity wins out over imagination.' Sergiovanni

3. The central problem of an education based on experience is to select the kind of present experiences that live fruitfully and creatively in subsequent experience.' John Dewey

4. 'The curriculum is to be thought of in terms activity and experience rather than knowledge to be acquired and facts to be stored.' Haddow Report UK 1931
    a. Curriculum means a written plan that includes:
    b. The goals for children's development and learning;
    c. The experiences through which they will achieve these goals;
    d. What staff and parents do to help children achieve these goals; and
    e. The materials needed to support the implementation of the curriculum."
    Head Start Program Performance Standards

5. Young children cannot think very well when they sit silently. However, movement, manipulation, and noise in themselves are not necessarily educational. The teacher who stops using worksheets is taking a step in the right direction, but this is only the first step. We must replace the worksheets with an environment that offers ample opportunities for children to think as they manipulate objects." **Connie Williams and Constance Kamii in "How do young children learn by handling objects?"** *Young Children, Volume 42***, Number 1, 1986.**

6. **Schools** need to illustrate the connection between curriculum and the real world. Students can spout back lessons but they don't know what it means.
    John Williams quotes

7. 'Much of the material presented in schools strikes students as alien, if not pointless.' **Howard Gardner**

8. "..teachers talk of consolidation rather than challenge...they (students) tend to become bored and uninspired" (Barber, 1999).

9. "Students who reject (for any reason) the school's values are generally labelled alienated or disengaged...we find that if a student is engaged then the teacher is responsible..but if the student is disengaged then the problem is with the student.." (Zyngier, 2007).

Chapter 6
TeXes Principal Competency 5

Données ISD
298302 Analysis Drive
Rigor, TX 76392

Dear New Principal,

I want to thank you for your willingness to serve in the capacity of temporary Principal of Margaret Spellings Elementary School during Principal Davis' absence. Prior to Principal Davis' untimely absence to due to illness, she was heavily engaged in reviewing school data obtained from a comprehensive needs assessment that will be used to develop the schools' Campus Improvement Plan. As you are aware, Texas Education Code requires the principal of each school campus, with the assistance of the campus-level committee to develop, review, and revise the campus improvement plan for the purpose of improving student performance for all student populations, including students in special education programs. The Campus Improvement Plan must:

- Assess the academic achievement for each student in the school using the academic excellence indicator system
- Set the campus performance objectives based on the academic excellence indicator system, including objectives for special needs populations, including students in special education programs
- Identify how the campus goals will be met for each student;
- Determine the resources needed to implement the plan;
- Identify staff needed to implement the plan;
- Set timelines for reaching the goals;
- Measure progress toward the performance objectives periodically to ensure that the plan is resulting in academic improvement;
- Include goals and methods for violence prevention and intervention on campus;
- Provide for a program to encourage parental involvement at the campus.

In Principal Davis's absence, you will be expected to provide the leadership needed to complete the Campus Improvement Plan. The campus level planning committee members have been selected and are ready to begin this important work. To help support innovative and out of the box thinking—I am pleased to announce that Margaret Spellings was granted a federal grant of $2.5 million to improve academic achievement for the upcoming academic school year. As you are developing this plan- the sky is the limit when developing activities—improved student academic achievement is the goal! Should you need assistance, please do not hesitate to contact my office.

Dr. Tamla Jones-Brown
Superintendent
Donnees ISD

71

MARGARET SPELLINGS ELEMENTARY SCHOOL

Margaret Spellings Elementary School is a low socioeconomic campus. Margaret Spellings Elementary School is a neighborhood school with an average enrollment of 490 children. Spellings has approximately 99.6 % Title 1 at risk students. These at risk categories include students who are free and reduced lunch, homeless, and not achieving academically. The majority of students identified as at risk have failed a State or District assessment, are limited English Proficient, or have repeated a grade. Approximately 80% of the population is African American, 17% are Hispanic, and 3% are White. Of the 16 students identified as Gifted and Talented, 2 are African American, 6 Hispanic and 8 are White.

For this case, you will be presented with school data obtained from a variety of sources that will help to inform the goals needed to complete the Campus Improvement Plan. All data presented are valuable and should be carefully reviewed and analyzed. The Principal in Texas knows how to advocate, nurture, and sustain an instructional program and a campus culture that are conducive to student learning and staff professional growth. Your work on this case should demonstrate that you have an understanding and mastery of:

Facilitating the development of a campus learning organization that supports instructional improvement and change through ongoing study of relevant research and best practice.

Facilitating the implementation of sound, research-based instructional strategies, decisions, and programs in which multiple opportunities to learn and be successful are available to all students.

Creating conditions that encourage staff, students, families/caregivers, and the community to strive to achieve the campus vision.

Ensuring that all students are provided high-quality, flexible instructional programs with appropriate resources and services to meet individual student needs.

Using formative and summative student assessment data to develop, support, and improve campus instructional strategies and goals.

Facilitating the use and integration of technology, telecommunications, and information systems to enhance learning.

Facilitating the implementation of sound, research-based theories and techniques of teaching, learning, classroom management, student discipline, and school safety to ensure a campus environment conducive to teaching and learning.

Facilitating the development, implementation, evaluation, and refinement of student services and activity programs to fulfill academic, developmental, social, and cultural needs.

Analyzing instructional needs and allocate resources effectively and equitably.

Analyzing the implications of various factors (e.g., staffing patterns, class scheduling formats, school organizational structures, student discipline practices) for teaching and learning.

Ensuring responsiveness to diverse sociological, linguistic, cultural, and other factors that may affect students' development and learning.

TEXAS EDUCATION AGENCY
Accountability Summary
Margaret Spelling Elementary School

Accountability Rating

Improvement Required

Met Standards on	Did Not Meet Standards on
- Student Achievement	- Closing Performance Gaps
- Student Progress	

Performance Index Report

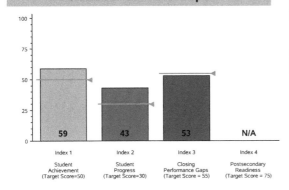

	Index 1	Index 2	Index 3	Index 4
	59	43	53	N/A
	Student Achievement (Target Score=50)	Student Progress (Target Score=30)	Closing Performance Gaps (Target Score = 55)	Postsecondary Readiness (Target Score = 75)

Performance Index Summary

Index	Points Earned	Maximum Points	Index Score
1 - Student Achievement	229	390	59
2 - Student Progress	430	1,000	43
3 - Closing Performance Gaps	319	600	53
4 - Postsecondary Readiness	N/A	N/A	N/A

Distinction Designation

Academic Achievement in Reading/ELA
Percent of Eligible Measures in Top Quartile
1 out of 4 = 25%

DOES NOT QUALIFY

Academic Achievement in Mathematics
Percent of Eligible Measures in Top Quartile
2 out of 3 = 67%

DOES NOT QUALIFY

Top 25 Percent Student Progress
DOES NOT QUALIFY

Campus Demographics

Campus Type	Elementary
Campus Size	492 Students
Grade Span	PK - 05
Percent Economically Disadvantaged	99.6%
Percent English Language Learners	39.6%
Mobility Rate	31.0%

System Safeguards

Number and Percent of Indicators Met

Performance Rates	16 out of 17 = 94%
Participation Rates	10 out of 10 = 100%
Graduation Rates	N/A
Total	**26 out of 27 = 96%**

School Campus: Margare Spellings

	General Fund	%	Per Student	All Funds	%	Per Student
Expenditures by Object (Objects 6100-6600)						
Total Expenditures	2,660,185	100.00	6,395	3,093,952	100.00	7,437
Operating-Payroll	2,416,579	90.84	5,809	2,619,751	84.67	6,297
Other Operating	242,310	9.11	582	472,905	15.28	1,137
Non-Operating(Equipt/Supplies)	1,296	0.05	3	1,296	0.04	3
Expenditures by Function (Objects 6100-6400 Only)						
Total Operating Expenditures	2,658,889	100.00	6,392	3,092,656	100.00	7,434
Instruction (11,95) *	1,890,856	71.11	4,545	2,015,312	65.16	4,845
Instructional Res/Media (12) *	70,382	2.65	169	70,382	2.28	169
Curriculum/Staff Develop (13) *	24,678	0.93	59	42,422	1.37	102
Instructional Leadership (21) *	43,557	1.64	105	44,284	1.43	106
School Leadership (23) *	177,574	6.68	427	178,537	5.77	429
Guidance/Counseling Svcs (31) *	83,466	3.14	201	83,466	2.70	201
Social Work Services (32) *	3,717	0.14	9	3,717	0.12	9
Health Services (33) *	63,910	2.40	154	63,910	2.07	154
Food (35) **	0	0.00	0	282,104	9.12	678
Extracurricular (36) *	0	0.00	0	0	0.00	0
Plant Maint/Operation (51) * **	300,749	11.31	723	308,522	9.98	742
Security/Monitoring (52) * **	0	0.00	0	0	0.00	0
Data Processing Svcs (53)* **	0	0.00	0	0	0.00	0
Program expenditures by Program (Objects 6100-6400 only)						
Total Operating Expenditures	2,142,659	100.00	5,151	2,286,549	100.00	5,497
Regular	1,814,376	84.68	4,361	1,814,526	79.36	4,362
Gifted & Talented	40,955	1.91	98	40,955	1.79	98
Career & Technical	0	0.00	0	0	0.00	0
Students with Disabilities	99,252	4.63	239	99,252	4.34	239
Accelerated Education	244	0.01	1	56,546	2.47	136
Bilingual	65,887	3.08	158	65,887	2.88	158
Nondisc Alted-AEP Basic Serv	0	0.00	0	0	0.00	0
Disc Alted-DAEP Basic Serv	0	0.00	0	0	0.00	0
Disc Alted-DAEP Supplemental	0	0.00	0	0	0.00	0
T1 A Schoolwide-St Comp >=40%	121,945	5.69	293	209,383	9.16	503
Athletic Programming	0	0.00	0	0	0.00	0
High School Allotment	0	0.00	0	0	0.00	0

Note: Some amounts may not total due to rounding.

RESULTS FROM CLIMATE NEEDS ASSESSMENT

Of the teachers surveyed, 25% feel the school the school is safe, clean, has enough learning space and all races and cultures are respected. The staff is given the vision and mission statement at the beginning of the school year. About half of the staff agrees that the school forms relationships, shows respect towards each other and generally works as a team. Approximately 13% of the students polled indicated they were involved in extracurricular activities.

CLIMATE NEEDS

- Teachers need to be more proactive with dealing with student issues.
- Make available more extracurricular activities for students to participate in.
- Implement Conscious Discipline throughout the school to improve school climate.
- Staff would like more input into decision-making
- A need for a well-focused and well implemented campus wide discipline and incentive system and a plan to increase parent involvement.
- The perception of some staff showed a need for better communication from leadership regarding school events in a more visible location.
- Students need to show more empathy
- School wide training on bullying
- Fair treatment of all staff
- There were 237 discipline referrals for the school year. The majority of them came from fourth and fifth grades.
- Professional Development for School Climate (How to Improve Our School Climate)
- More parent support

CAMPUS IMPROVEMENT PLAN
PLANNING TEMPLATE
CLIMATE

CLIMATE GOALS:

Strategy Description	Staff Responsible for Monitoring	Evidence that Demonstrates Success	Formative Reviews			
			Nov	Jan	Mar	June
1)			☐	☐	☐	☐
2)			☐	☐	☐	☐
3)			☐	☐	☐	☐
4)			☐	☐	☐	☐
5)			☐	☐	☐	☐

✘ = Discontinue   ◯ = No Progress   ◑ = Some Progress   ◕ = Considerable   ✔ = Accomplished

CAMPUS IMPROVEMENT PLANNING BUDGET	
RESOURCE	AMOUNT
	$
	$
	$
	$
	$
	$
	$
	$
	$
	$
	$
TOTAL	$

Professional development is aligned to District initiatives and is delivered on Staff Development days, during the school day, or after school depending on need. Relevant professional development is available for all personnel depending on individual need. Implementation of professional learning is monitored using walkthrough data. All teachers are evaluated each year using the PDAS. Teachers whose performance is below district or state standards are placed on a growth plan. Teachers with strong instructional practices mentor other teachers and/or model effective teaching practices. Teachers work and plan in teams and share ideas regularly. All teachers are focused on improving student performance.

STAFF QUALITY AND RETENTION NEEDS

- The staff retention rate is 55%. There were fifteen teachers that left at the end of the school year. Twenty professional staff members will be new to their positions on the campus.
- All teachers are not highly qualified.
- A conscious effort to build instructional support and administrative teams that function to their fullest ability.
- We need to maintain a good strong Administrative Team and a good, strong faculty and staff.
- We need to have a plan as to how we can maintain quality staff.
- We need stability for everyone.
- We need to work closely with PTA so that we will have more parent volunteers in the school.
- We need to all be trained in Conflict Resolution so that we can better equip our students.
- Five emergency ESL certified teachers need to complete requirements to be certified.
- Training in guided math/reading strategies for more individualized targeted instruction and training in technology Integration
- High retention rate of faculty and staff
- Ample professional development opportunities in the summer, during the school year and through on-line courses
- A strong and supportive curriculum department that is supportive of teachers and campuses.
- Variety of Effective Recruitment Processes.
- Strong District Mentor Program
- Planning time to write, develop and reflect

STAFF GOALS:

Strategy Description	Staff Responsible for Monitoring	Evidence that Demonstrates Success	Formative Reviews			
			Nov	Jan	Mar	June
1)						
2)						
3)						
4)						
5)						

✗ = Discontinue ● = No Progress ◑ = Some Progress ◕ = Considerable ✓ = Accomplished

CAMPUS IMPROVEMENT PLANNING BUDGET	
RESOURCE	AMOUNT
	$
	$
	$
	$
	$
	$
	$
	$
	$
	$
	$
TOTAL	$

RESULTS FROM CURRICULUM, INSTRUCTION AND ASSESSMENT NEEDS ASSESSMENT

Curriculum is linked to the TEKS and other standards for learning by the use of weekly lesson plans, posted objectives, child-friendly objectives, C-Scope curriculum, District Based Assessments (DBAs), and test scores. Through integration of problem solving, critical thinking, creative thinking, and the embedding of technology into the lessons, 21st century learning skills are being taught.

To measure student achievement, students are given a variety of assessments. On this campus we use, teacher made assessments, district based assessments, and work samples. Interventions are based on data from assessments and are provided by our pull out teachers and paid tutors.

Instructional strategies vary by teacher and are somewhat driven by data. Teachers are trying interventions in the classroom and are currently working on ways to document the effectiveness of individual interventions. The teachers are also trying various methods of data collection to ensure students success.

CURRICULUM NEEDS

- Provide Professional Development to ensure rigor and high quality instruction.
- Additional time for teachers to meet to evaluate the needs of students and make curriculum adjustments
- Additional personnel needed for small group instruction, intervention, and differentiation
- Continual work is needed to provide curriculum alignment with assessments including DBAs
- Increased planning between classroom teacher and special education teachers
- Additional personnel to assist with small group instruction, interventions and modifications
- Increasing technology usage in the classroom to engage students
- Providing teachers with planning time to analyze data and address different student groups provide training to increase instructional strategies, new curriculum and initiatives
- Incorporating critical writing
- Creating high-rigor reading lessons
- Meeting the needs of the advanced learner through differentiation of instruction
- Use data to determine type and duration of interventions
- Use goal setting strategies for student involvement in the learning process
- We need more cohesiveness in our planning among grade levels and among content areas.
- We also need to ensure that students are setting goals for themselves in the content areas.

CURRICULUM, INSTRUCTION AND ASSESSMENT GOALS:

Strategy Description	Staff Responsible for Monitoring	Evidence that Demonstrates Success	Formative Reviews			
			Nov	Jan	Mar	June
1)						
2)						
3)						
4)						
5)						

X = Discontinue ● = No Progress ● = Some Progress ● = Considerable ✓ = Accomplished

CAMPUS IMPROVEMENT PLANNING BUDGET	
RESOURCE	AMOUNT
	$
	$
	$
	$
	$
	$
	$
	$
	$
	$
	$
TOTAL	$

Community members are involved in many activities to support student learning Parents generally feel welcome. Parents are always welcome to have lunch with their children; we have several lunch visitors on a daily basis. A parent involvement committee was established in the beginning of the year and 1 parent became involved in planning activities. Participation on this committee fluctuated through the year as work schedules changed.

FAMILY AND COMMUNITY INVOLVEMENT NEEDS

- Continued parent activities with possibly changing the time of activities to accommodate the schedules of busy parents will positively impact the percentage of parental involvement.
- We need to provide more academic resources for parents to help students at home.
- We need to have more Academic Nights initiated by grade levels to teach parents effective strategies to improve student performance in reading and math at all grade levels.
- We need to provide Parent training on effective strategies for disciplining, temper tantrums, health issues, and communicating with their children.
- Better communication in Spanish
- More consistent communication through student folders
- More opportunities for parent volunteers to assist during the instructional day and during family events
- Frequent and consistent updating of website
- Increasing avenues for teachers to communicate with parents
- Explore additional ways to increase parents' understanding of academic expectations and provide more resources to improve their ability to help their children.
- Ensure all newsletters and phone messages are distributed in the native languages of our parents who have yet to learned to read English.

CAMPUS IMPROVEMENT PLAN
PLANNING TEMPLATE
FAMILY COMMUNITY INVOLVEMENT

PARENTAL AND COMMUNITY ENGAGEMENT GOALS:

Strategy Description	Staff Responsible for Monitoring	Evidence that Demonstrates Success	Formative Reviews			
			Nov	Jan	Mar	June
1)			☐	☐	☐	☐
2)			☐	☐	☐	☐
3)			☐	☐	☐	☐
4)			☐	☐	☐	☐
5)			☐	☐	☐	☐

✗ = Discontinue ● = No Progress ● = Some Progress ● = Considerable ✓ = Accomplished

CAMPUS IMPROVEMENT PLANNING BUDGET	
RESOURCE	AMOUNT
	$
	$
	$
	$
	$
	$
	$
	$
	$
	$
	$
TOTAL	$

RESULTS FROM TECHNOLOGY NEEDS ASSESSMENT

Technology is extremely limited and outdated. Technology is essential in the daily life of students as well as staff. Our campus staff has a willingness to use and seek training on unfamiliar software and hardware supplied by the district.

TECHNOLOGY NEEDS

- Hardware is very limited
- Current technology does not meet the needs of students and staff.
- All teachers need access to a projection device, student iPads, and computers.
- Software licenses are limited in comparison to the large student body.
- Students need basic computer application lessons on how to use various programs.
- Teachers and staff need training on iPads, apps, and how to use the iPads as other devices, clickers, e-readers, etc. in their daily instruction. They also need training on how to effectively use the data from the software applications.
- Tech support is limited.
- Technology Integration training (i.e, creating student-led presentations, ideas for using iPads in the classroom)
- Increasing rigor-level through the use of technology to help apply what students are learning through projects
- Teachers using technology to improve instruction by learning ways to have students engaged in using technology during lessons.
- Additional classroom computers with a larger capacity are needed to run programs such as Think Through Math and IStation.
- Istation for reading
- Keyboarding skills and basic proficiencies need to be taught to the students.
- Professional development for the integration of technology into lessons.
- More integration by the students of technology in their learning.
- Support for the teachers to learn how to use their technology that they have.
- Our outdated equipment that is in need of continuous repair is a huge barrier in preventing the use of effective technology.
- The unreliable link to the internet is also a problem which inhibits our instructional delivery.
- Improved internet speed-the internet speed is causing too much delay in the delivery of valuable instructional time.
- More Success Maker Five licenses are needed to improve student performance.

CAMPUS IMPROVEMENT PLAN
PLANNING TEMPLATE
TECHNOLOGY

TECHNOLOGY GOALS:

Strategy Description	Staff Responsible for Monitoring	Evidence that Demonstrates Success	Formative Reviews			
			Nov	Jan	Mar	June
1)			☐	☐	☐	☐
2)			☐	☐	☐	☐
3)			☐	☐	☐	☐
4)			☐	☐	☐	☐
5)			☐	☐	☐	☐

✖ = Discontinue　● = No Progress　◖ = Some Progress　◕ = Considerable　✔ = Accomplished

CAMPUS IMPROVEMENT PLANNING BUDGET	
RESOURCE	AMOUNT
	$
	$
	$
	$
	$
	$
	$
	$
	$
	$
	$
	$
TOTAL	$

RESULTS FROM STUDENT ACHIEVEMENT NEEDS ASSESSMENT

STAAR results for ALL students reflect the following passing rates:

3rd Grade Math - 30%	4th Grade Writing - 65%
3rd Grade Reading - 54%	5th Grade Math - 55%
4th Grade Math - 25%	5th Grade Reading - 45%
4th Grade Reading - 45%	5th Grade Science - 35%

STAAR results for economically disadvantaged students reflect the following passing rates:

3rd Grade Math - 3%
3rd Grade Reading - 25%
4th Grade Math - 5%
4th Grade Reading - 35%
4th Grade Writing - 20%
5th Grade Math - 15%

STUDENT ACHIEVEMENT NEEDS

- Improvement is needed in all content areas at all grade levels
- Discrepancy between report card grades and STAAR performance indicates a need to look at the rigor of graded student work.
- Our instruction needs to match the rigor level of the state TEKS so that students can be successful in all areas.
- Additional professional development to better meet the needs of LEP students and male students: Thinking Maps training to increase students' vocabulary development, abstract and inferential thinking; Additional professional development in differentiated instruction
- Additional training in accommodation, modification and models of service for special education students.
- On site math coaching to build teacher capacity in mathematics
- African-American students need significant improvement in reading and mathematics
- Science needs more depth of instruction at the lower grades
- Percent of African American students passing math in grades three, four, and five was well below the percent of Hispanic and White students passing math.
- An increase in the rigor level of our instructional program will address our student achievement needs.
- Vertical team planning along with grade level planning
- Professional Learning Committee (PLC) meetings should be aligned to student needs.

CAMPUS IMPROVEMENT PLAN
PLANNING TEMPLATE
STUDENT ACHIEVEMENT

STUDENT ACHIEVEMENT GOALS:

	Strategy Description	Staff Responsible for Monitoring	Evidence that Demonstrates Success	Formative Reviews			
				Nov	Jan	Mar	June
1)							
2)							
3)							
4)							
5)							

X = Discontinue   ● = No Progress   ◗ = Some Progress   ● = Considerable   ✓ = Accomplished

CAMPUS IMPROVEMENT PLANNING BUDGET	
RESOURCE	AMOUNT
	$
	$
	$
	$
	$
	$
	$
	$
	$
	$
	$
TOTAL	$

SUPPLEMENTARY RESOURCES
CHAPTER SIX
COMPETENCY FIVE

Books

Wilmore, E. L. (2013). *Passing the Special Education TExES Exam*. Corwin Press.

Texas Public School Organization and Administration: 2012 [Misc. Supplies] VORNBERG JAMES A (Author), CONSILIENCE LLC (Author), BORGEMENKE ARTHUR J (Author)

Ainscow, M., Beresford, J., Harris, A., Hopkins, D., Southworth, G., & West, M. (2013). *Creating the conditions for school improvement: a handbook of staff development activities*. Routledge.

Bauer, S. C., & Brazer, S. D. (2011). *Using research to lead school improvement: Turning evidence into action*. Sage.

Bernhardt, V. (2013). *Data analysis for continuous school improvement*. Routledge.

Cribb, M., & Woods, D. (Eds.). (2012). *Effective LEAs and school improvement*. Routledge.

Davies, B., & Ellison, L. (2013). *The new strategic direction and development of the school: Key frameworks for school improvement planning*. Routledge.

Davies, B., & Ellison, L. (2013). *The new strategic direction and development of the school: Key frameworks for school improvement planning*. Routledge.

Dimmock, C. (Ed.). (2013). *School-based management and school effectiveness*. Routledge.

Visscher, A. J., & Coe, R. (Eds.). (2013). *School improvement through performance feedback* (Vol. 10). Routledge.

Articles

Adelman, H., & Taylor, L. (2011). What Do Principals Say about Their Work? Implications for Addressing Barriers to Learning and School Improvement. *Center for Mental Health in Schools at UCLA*.

Bean, R. M., & Dagen, A. S. (Eds.). (2011). *Best Practices of Literacy Leaders: Keys to School Improvement*. Guilford Press.

Bryk, A. S. (2010). Organizing schools for improvement. *Phi Delta Kappan*, *91*(7), 23-30.

Dunaway, D. M., Kim, D. H., & Szad, E. R. (2012, April). Perceptions of the purpose and value of the school improvement plan process. In *The Educational Forum* (Vol. 76, No. 2, pp. 158-173). Taylor & Francis Group.

Websites and Blogs

http://www.schoolimprovement.com
http://www.tea.state.tx.us
http://www.corestandards.org
http://pdkintl.org/publications/kappan/
http://www.edweek.org/ew/index.html
http://www.naesp.org
http://learningforward.org/publications/learning-principal#.UxpZXxbog4M
http://www.wallacefoundation.org/Pages/default.aspx

Reports

School Improvement Planning: What's Missing?
http://smhp.psych.ucla.edu/pdfdocs/schoolimprovement/whatsmissing.pdf

Successful Schools: From Research to Action Plans
http://www.leadered.com/pdf/Successful%20Schools%206-05.pdf

Achieving Dramatic School Improvement: An Exploratory Study
https://www2.ed.gov/rschstat/eval/other/dramatic-school-improvement/exploratory-study.pdf

YouTube Videos

School Improvement Plan Presentation
Link
http://youtu.be/6CzMY7Exoyw
Embed
<iframe width="420" height="315" src="//www.youtube.com/embed/6CzMY7Exoyw" frameborder="0" allowfullscreen></iframe>)

Webinar - Intensive Support for Struggling Schools: Improving-Douglas Reeves
Link

http://youtu.be/PsIp6XUcorA
Embed
<iframe width="420" height="315" src="//www.youtube.com/embed/PsIp6XUcorA" frameborder="0" allowfullscreen></iframe>)

Heidi Hayes Jacobs: "21st Century Teaching & Learning within the Common Core"
Link
http://youtu.be/xvOnha7XnaQ
Embed
<iframe width="560" height="315" src="//www.youtube.com/embed/xvOnha7XnaQ" frameborder="0" allowfullscreen></iframe>)

Heidi Hayes Jacobs - What is Curriculum Mapping
Link
http://youtu.be/8etEUVzo2GE
Embed
<iframe width="420" height="315" src="//www.youtube.com/embed/8etEUVzo2GE" frameborder="0" allowfullscreen></iframe>)

Michael Fullan on what school reform is…
Link
http://youtu.be/bxjLqHphsVY
Embed
<iframe width="560" height="315" src="//www.youtube.com/embed/bxjLqHphsVY" frameborder="0" allowfullscreen></iframe>)

Mini Projects/Additional Assignments

Create a PowerPoint Presentation outlining the Campus Improvement Plan to the school community.

Create a PowerPoint Presentation for the School Board highlighting the top three goals for each category of the Campus Improvement Plan.

Create a PowerPoint Presentation for the student population highlighting the goals of the Campus Improvement Plan

Create a Newsletter highlighting the key goals of the Campus Improvement Plan

Create a webpage highlighting key improvement goals and objectives of the Campus Improvement Plan

You have been granted unlimited funds to improve student achievement. Create a Campus Improvement Plan based on the data provided in this case study.

Discussion/Reflection Topics

1. "The main aim of the facilitative leader is to leverage the resources of group members."
   —Ingrid Bens

2. "The facilitator's job is to *support everyone to do their best thinking*. To do this, the facilitator encourages full participation, promotes mutual understanding, and cultivates shared responsibility."
   —Sam Kaner

3. "Perhaps one of the most difficult things for a facilitator to do is to allow someone to struggle. To rescue people from the struggle immediately shuts off an opportunity for them to learn and grow. Supporting and encouraging them through the struggle is much more rewarding for everyone involved."
   —Trevor Bentley

4. "It is a misuse of our power to take responsibility for solving problems that belong to others."
   —Peter Block

5. Strategic planning is a rational planning process, but it has strong psychological effects on an organization and the people involved in the process.
   -Dr Shirley McCune

6. Providing people with data *before* asking for their opinions and ideas about what schools should do leads to different responses and outcomes.
   -Dr Shirley McCune

7. The biggest risk is not taking any risk... In a world that changing really quickly, the only strategy that is guaranteed to fail is not taking risks.
   -Mark Zuckerberg

8. Leadership is a potent combination of strategy and character. But if you must be without one, be without the strategy.
   -Norman Schwarzkopf

9. There's only one growth strategy: work hard.
   -William Hague

10. Success doesn't necessarily come from breakthrough innovation but from flawless execution. A great strategy alone won't win a game or a battle; the win comes from basic blocking and tackling. – Neveen Jain

Chapter 7
TeXes Principal Competency 6

(Photo: By Patricia Brach (This image is from the FEMA Photo Library.) [Public domain], via Wikimedia Commons)

Charlotte Danielson School of Excellence, Diversity and Exceptionality
836362 Instruction Drive
Blooms, TX 472920

Welcome New Assistant Principal,

I am very pleased and excited that you have accepted the position of Assistant Principal at the Danielson School of Excellence. The Danielson School has experienced major changes over the last year and the replacement of the entire administrative team probably tops the list. As a new administrative team, we will need to proceed carefully, understanding that the entire school community is adjusting to this change. With that being said, we must still forge forward in turning this school around. There are clear obstacles and challenges but none are insurmountable.

Fortunately, I was able to access staff evaluations for all staff members from last school year. I have arranged for our entire administrative team to meet for a working lunch to discuss how we will build the capacity of the staff. Agenda items for our working lunch will be:

1. Strategize on how we will implement a staff evaluation and development system to improve the performance of all staff members
2. Develop an implementation plan to identify the appropriate models for supervision and staff development, while ensuring compliance with the legal requirements for personnel management in the state of Texas.
3. Review of current lesson planning template currently used.

If you wish to add to this agenda please advise ASAP so that the agenda items can be updated and shared with the entire team.

I have divided the evaluation documents equally among the entire team. You have been assigned to review grades 6-8 regular and special education teacher formal and informal evaluations as well as samples of completed lesson plans. Attached for your review are ten formal teacher observations, four informal teacher walkthrough observation feedback forms and two lesson plans. Please review and be prepared to present and discuss your recommendations for staff development, teacher improvement plans and teacher formal and informal observation schedules.

Based on my cursory review of the teacher observation forms and lesson plans, it appears that the prior administrative team were using the Charlotte Danielson Teacher Observation Framework to conduct observations and teachers used the Understanding by Design Backwards Lesson Planning Model. It is not clear at this time the level fidelity of which these frameworks were implemented. Therefore, we will want to review these models to determine if they best meet the needs of our teachers and our students.

Should you have questions or need to contact me, I can be reached at 932-383-3293 cell, home number 382-382-3892 and email mary.hunter-mendez@cdisd.org.

Dr. Madeline Jane Hunter-Mendez
Principal

Charlotte Danielson School of Excellence

Charlotte Danielson School of Excellence has been identified as a chronically failing school that is located in one of the poorest rural communities in the state of Texas. There are approximately 670 students, 98% of the student population is economically disadvantaged; 70% of the students are Hispanic; 97% of the student population is considered at-risk because they are struggling academically or behaviorally, are LEP learners, have been retained, are homeless, or receive Special Education services. To further exacerbate the unique challenges of this school, 25% of the students are under the care of the State of Texas and are currently in foster homes. Classroom sizes are not ideal and space availability continues as a challenge. Student, administrator and teacher mobility rates continue to increase each year. Special student populations such as Gifted an Talented and Special Education students are under identified and thus do not receive supports necessary for success. The Danielson School has failed to meet Adequate Yearly Progress for the last decade and is considered one of the worst performing schools in the State of Texas and in the United States.

For this case you will need to provide support to your Principal. You are being asked to review teacher performance evaluations, informal walkthroughs and copies of lesson plans that were conducted in the prior year. Your task will be to review all of these documents carefully to provide your Principal with recommendations for creating a professional development plan to build capacity of staff to turn the building around. In this activity you will need to demonstrate your understanding and mastery of the following:

Working collaboratively with other campus personnel to develop, implement, evaluate, and revise a comprehensive campus professional development plan that addresses staff needs and aligns professional development with identified goals.

Facilitating the application of adult learning principles and motivation theory to all campus professional development activities, including the use of appropriate content, processes, and contexts.

Allocating appropriate time, funding, and other needed resources to ensure the effective implementation of professional development plans.

Implementing effective, appropriate, and legal strategies for the recruitment, screening, selection, assignment, induction, development, evaluation, promotion, discipline, and dismissal of campus staff.

Using formative and summative evaluation procedures to enhance the knowledge and skills of campus staff.

Diagnosing campus organizational health and morale and implement strategies to provide ongoing support to campus staff.

Engaging in ongoing professional development activities to enhance one's own knowledge and skills and to model lifelong learning.

TEXAS EDUCATION AGENCY
Accountability Summary

Accountability Rating
Improvement Required

Met Standards on	Did Not Meet Standards on
- Student Progress	- Student Achievement
	- Closing Performance Gaps

Performance Index Report

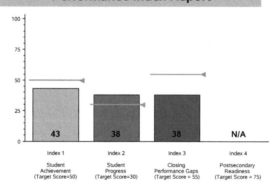

43	Index 1 — Student Achievement (Target Score=50)
38	Index 2 — Student Progress (Target Score=30)
38	Index 3 — Closing Performance Gaps (Target Score = 55)
N/A	Index 4 — Postsecondary Readiness (Target Score = 75)

Performance Index Summary

Index	Points Earned	Maximum Points	Index Score
1 - Student Achievement	268	627	43
2 - Student Progress	537	1,400	38
3 - Closing Performance Gaps	230	600	38
4 - Postsecondary Readiness	N/A	N/A	N/A

Distinction Designation

Academic Achievement in Reading/ELA
Percent of Eligible Measures in Top Quartile
0 out of 4 = 0%
DOES NOT QUALIFY

Academic Achievement in Mathematics
Percent of Eligible Measures in Top Quartile
0 out of 3 = 0%
DOES NOT QUALIFY

Top 25 Percent Student Progress
DOES NOT QUALIFY

Campus Demographics

Campus Type	Elementary
Campus Size	676 Students
Grade Span	EE - 05
Percent Economically Disadvantaged	98.2%
Percent English Language Learners	57.0%
Mobility Rate	20.3%

System Safeguards

Number and Percent of Indicators Met

Performance Rates	5 out of 20 = 25%
Participation Rates	12 out of 12 = 100%
Graduation Rates	N/A
Total	**17 out of 32 = 53%**

School Campus: Charlotte Danielson

	General Fund	%	Per Student	All Funds	%	Per Student
Expenditures by Object (Objects 6100-6600)						
Total Expenditures	5,545,236	100.00	5,956	6,414,446	100.00	6,890
Operating-Payroll	5,093,184	91.85	5,471	5,674,298	88.46	6,095
Other Operating	415,764	7.50	447	684,079	10.66	735
Non-Operating(Equipt/Supplies)	36,288	0.65	39	56,069	0.87	60
Expenditures by Function (Objects 6100-6400 Only)						
Total Operating Expenditures	5,508,948	100.00	5,917	6,358,377	100.00	6,830
Instruction (11,95) *	3,884,172	70.51	4,172	4,227,201	66.48	4,540
Instructional Res/Media (12) *	125,182	2.27	134	126,944	2.00	136
Curriculum/Staff Develop (13) *	52,322	0.95	56	243,730	3.83	262
Instructional Leadership (21) *	87,101	1.58	94	87,101	1.37	94
School Leadership (23) *	522,839	9.49	562	537,783	8.46	578
Guidance/Counseling Svcs (31) *	288,859	5.24	310	292,385	4.60	314
Social Work Services (32) *	9,585	0.17	10	9,585	0.15	10
Health Services (33) *	110,528	2.01	119	111,696	1.76	120
Food (35) **	0	0.00	0	273,930	4.31	294
Extracurricular (36) *	38,548	0.70	41	38,548	0.61	41
Plant Maint/Operation (51) * **	350,121	6.36	376	368,626	5.80	396
Security/Monitoring (52) * **	39,691	0.72	43	40,848	0.64	44
Data Processing Svcs (53)* **	0	0.00	0	0	0.00	0
Program expenditures by Program (Objects 6100-6400 only)						
Total Operating Expenditures	5,080,588	100.00	5,457	5,636,403	100.00	6,054
Regular	3,451,130	67.93	3,707	3,451,130	61.23	3,707
Gifted & Talented	34,730	0.68	37	34,730	0.62	37
Career & Technical	71,736	1.41	77	71,736	1.27	77
Students with Disabilities	986,091	19.41	1,059	1,003,327	17.80	1,078
Accelerated Education	24,002	0.47	26	305,582	5.42	328
Bilingual	90,802	1.79	98	91,113	1.62	98
Nondisc Alted-AEP Basic Serv	0	0.00	0	0	0.00	0
Disc Alted-DAEP Basic Serv	0	0.00	0	0	0.00	0
Disc Alted-DAEP Supplemental	0	0.00	0	0	0.00	0
T1 A Schoolwide-St Comp >=40%	422,097	8.31	453	678,785	12.04	729
Athletic Programming	0	0.00	0	0	0.00	0
High School Allotment	0	0.00	0	0	0.00	0

Note: Some amounts may not total due to rounding.

TEXAS EDUCATION AGENCY
2Student Achievement Data Table
Charlotte Danieleson

STAAR Performance

	All Students	African American	Hispanic	White	American Indian	Asian	Pacific Islander	Two or More Races	Special Ed	Econ Disadv	ELL
All Subjects											
Percent of Tests											
% at Phase-in 1 Level II or above	64%	59%	66%	47%	**	*	-	-	67%	63%	56%
% at Final Level II or above	21%	16%	23%	6%	**	*	-	-	40%	20%	14%
% at Level III Advanced	4%	3%	4%	0%	**	*	-	-	6%	4%	2%
Number of Tests											
# at Phase-in 1 Level II or above	1,484	424	1,041	8	**	*	-	-	197	1,364	523
# at Final Level II or above	482	116	361	1	**	*	-	-	119	436	131
# at Level III Advanced	94	21	70	0	**	*	-	-	19	86	20
Total Tests	2,332	714	1,578	17	**	*	-	-	296	2,160	934
Reading											
Percent of Tests											
% at Phase-in 1 Level II or above	66%	63%	67%	*	*	*	-	-	68%	65%	54%
% at Final Level II or above	26%	21%	28%	*	*	*	-	-	38%	25%	16%
% at Level III Advanced	6%	5%	7%	*	*	*	-	-	6%	6%	2%
Number of Tests											
# at Phase-in 1 Level II or above	517	153	356	*	*	*	-	-	67	479	178
# at Final Level II or above	203	50	151	*	*	*	-	-	37	182	52
# at Level III Advanced	48	11	35	*	*	*	-	-	6	42	6
Total Tests	788	242	532	*	*	*	-	-	98	737	327
Mathematics											
Percent of Tests											
% at Phase-in 1 Level II or above	65%	56%	70%	*	*	*	-	-	68%	65%	62%
% at Final Level II or above	21%	15%	24%	*	*	*	-	-	41%	21%	15%
% at Level III Advanced	4%	2%	5%	*	*	*	-	-	10%	4%	4%
Number of Tests											
# at Phase-in 1 Level II or above	512	137	369	*	*	*	-	-	67	476	200
# at Final Level II or above	165	37	125	*	*	*	-	-	41	154	50
# at Level III Advanced	32	4	27	*	*	*	-	-	10	30	12
Total Tests	784	243	527	*	*	*	-	-	99	734	323
Writing											
Percent of Tests											
% at Phase-in 1 Level II or above	52%	49%	55%	*	*	*	-	-	64%	53%	46%
% at Final Level II or above	11%	13%	10%	*	*	*	-	-	45%	11%	7%
% at Level III Advanced	1%	4%	0%	*	*	*	-	-	9%	1%	1%
Number of Tests											
# at Phase-in 1 Level II or above	126	35	90	*	*	*	-	-	21	116	45
# at Final Level II or above	26	9	17	*	*	*	-	-	15	25	7
# at Level III Advanced	3	3	0	*	*	*	-	-	3	3	1
Total Tests	241	71	165	*	*	*	-	-	33	220	98

TEXAS EDUCATION AGENCY
Student Achievement Data Table
Charlotte Danieleson

2013 STAAR Performance

	All Students	African American	Hispanic	White	American Indian	Asian	Pacific Islander	Two or More Races	Special Ed	Econ Disadv	ELL
Science											
Percent of Tests											
% at Phase-in 1 Level II or above	64%	61%	66%	*	*	*	-	-	61%	62%	56%
% at Final Level II or above	18%	13%	21%	*	*	*	-	-	39%	18%	12%
% at Level III Advanced	1%	0%	2%	*	*	*	-	-	0%	1%	0%
Number of Tests											
# at Phase-in 1 Level II or above	166	48	116	*	*	*	-	-	20	145	52
# at Final Level II or above	47	10	37	*	*	*	-	-	13	41	11
# at Level III Advanced	3	0	3	*	*	*	-	-	0	3	0
Total Tests	259	79	177	*	*	*	-	-	33	234	93
Social Studies											
Percent of Tests											
% at Phase-in 1 Level II or above	63%	65%	62%	*	*	*	-	-	67%	63%	52%
% at Final Level II or above	16%	13%	18%	*	*	*	-	-	39%	14%	12%
% at Level III Advanced	3%	4%	3%	*	*	*	-	-	0%	3%	1%
Number of Tests											
# at Phase-in 1 Level II or above	163	51	110	*	*	*	-	-	22	148	48
# at Final Level II or above	41	10	31	*	*	*	-	-	13	34	11
# at Level III Advanced	8	3	5	*	*	*	-	-	0	8	1
Total Tests	260	79	177	*	*	*	-	-	33	235	93

TEXAS EDUCATION AGENCY
Closing Performance Gaps Data
Charlotte Danielson

	African American	Hispanic	White	American Indian	Asian	Pacific Islander	Two or More Races	
2012 STAAR Performance								
All Subjects - Used for Determining Lowest Performing Race/Ethnicity Group(s)								
Percent of Tests								
% at Phase-in 1 Level II or above	49%	60%	87%	*	*	-	*	
Number of Tests								
Total Tests	788	1,745	23	*	*	-	*	

	African American	Hispanic	White	American Indian	Asian	Pacific Islander	Two or More Races	Econ Disadv
2013 STAAR Performance								
Reading								
Percent of Tests								
% at Phase-in 1 Level II or above	64%	85%	*	*	*	-	-	73%
% at Final Level II or above	21%	47%	*	*	*	-	-	31%
% at Level III Advanced	5%	14%	*	*	*	-	-	9%
Number of Tests								
# at Phase-in 1 Level II or above	150	181	*	*	*	-	-	315
# at Final Level II or above	49	100	*	*	*	-	-	135
# at Level III Advanced	11	29	*	*	*	-	-	37
Total Tests	234	214	*	*	*	-	-	433
Mathematics								
Percent of Tests								
% at Phase-in 1 Level II or above	58%	80%	*	*	*	-	-	67%
% at Final Level II or above	15%	36%	*	*	*	-	-	25%
% at Level III Advanced	2%	7%	*	*	*	-	-	5%
Number of Tests								
# at Phase-in 1 Level II or above	136	170	*	*	*	-	-	290
# at Final Level II or above	36	76	*	*	*	-	-	108
# at Level III Advanced	4	15	*	*	*	-	-	20
Total Tests	235	213	*	*	*	-	-	434

LESSON SUMMARY

Objective (as written on the board):
Student Will Be Able To *define and provide examples of hazardous working conditions.*
Student Will Be Able To *write diary entry.*

Summary:
On the day of the observation, there were 32 students present. The desks were arranged in six cooperative groups. Mr. Shakespeare entered the classroom at approximately 8:30am. Students put down the chairs, opened the shades and the windows. The breakfast monitor went downstairs to pick up the breakfast. Students sat and their desks waiting patiently for their breakfast (students were not engaged in instructional activities during this time). Breakfast was delivered by the monitor at approximately 8:40am. Mr. Shakespeare instructed the students to go to the breakfast container to get their breakfast. Students adhered to Mr. Shakespeare's request; they selected their breakfast items and then returned to their respective desks. Mr. Shakespeare remained at his desk and talked on his cell phone at approximately 8:45am for about two minutes. Mr. Shakespeare went to the board to write the objective at 8:50. The following was written on the board

STUDENT WILL BE ABLE TO *define and provide examples of hazardous working conditions.*
STUDENT WILL BE ABLE TO *write a diary entry.*

At 8:59 Mr. Shakespeare informed the students that breakfast was over and that all breakfast containers had to be placed in the trash. Assigned students collected the breakfast garbage and then quickly disposed of the trash. Mr. Shakespeare then directed the students to clear off their desks and he handed out a worksheet. Additionally, students that had not completed their assignment from last Thursday in the computer lab were asked to go to the back of the classroom to the computer center to complete their missed assignment. Mr. Shakespeare provided students at the computer center with specific directions and instructions as to how to access the website and directions for completing the assignment. As Mr. Shakespeare provided directions to the five students seated at the computer the center, the remaining students sat patiently awaiting on Mr. Shakespeare's directions. Mr. Shakespeare redirected his attention to the students seated at their desks and he asked for the students who had completed both the back and front of the assignment sheet to raise their hands. Mr. Shakespeare provided the seated students with directions for completing their assignment. At 9:05 Mr. Shakespeare went back to his desk and worked on his computer as the students worked both at their desks and at the computer center. Several students asked Mr. Shakespeare questions about the assignment and Mr. Shakespeare immediately responded to their questions. Students

98

both at their desks and at the computer station were asked to complete the following questions

1. *The picture I want to share is*
2. *The working conditions were hazardous because..*
3. *Write a paragraph on the back of the paper about the picture your chose.*

While completing their assignments, students asked Mr. Shakespeare the following questions:

How do you find the hazardous working conditions?
What does child labor mean? Why do we have to put it on our paper?
What is it called when you get hurt at work and you get paid?
Are the students working in the factory slaves? (student asked the AP)

Mr. Shakespeare answered their questions from his desk.

At 9:23, Mr. Shakespeare walked to the back of the classroom to write on the large easel in the back of the classroom. He turned to a clean sheet clipped to the easel and then he went back to his desk and ate Wheat Thins. A student went to his desk to ask a question about the assignment, Mr. Shakespeare turned to his computer and pulled up the website to print out the picture which helped the student to complete his assignment.

At 9:29 Mr. Shakespeare then went back to the easel to write the following

Hazardous Working Conditions Fair Labor Standards Act (FLSA)
1. *Manufacturing and storing explosives*
2. *Driving a motor vehicle or being an outside helper on one*
3. *Coal Mining*
4. *Logging and saw milling*
5. *Power driven wood working machine*
6. *Mining, other than coal*
7. *Meat packing or processing*
8. *Wreaking and demolition and ship breaking operations.*

Students continued to work at their desks while Mr. Shakespeare completed writing on the easel—Mr. Shakespeare returned to his desk. At approximately 9:41am, Mr. Shakespeare asked students to get their literacy notebooks and to turn towards the back of the classroom to write down the items from the easel. Mr. Shakespeare went to the back of the room where the easel is located, reviewed each point (hazardous work conditions), prompted student discussion with low level questions as well as answered questions asked by the students. For example, Mr. Shakespeare asked students the following question:

1. *Do you think that it is wise for young kids to manufacture dynamite?*
2. *Everyone, do you know what a coal miner is?*

3. Do you know the dangers of coal mining?

Students also asked questions as Mr. Shakespeare reviewed each of the hazards listed on the easel:

*1. **What is dynamite***
*2. **What is sawmilling?***
*3. **Where do they make tooth picks?***
*4. **If you had $50 dollars back then would you be rich?***
*5. **Could you buy a house, a car with $50 dollars?***
*6. **Did they have little kids, like in the 2nd grade dropping out of school?***
*7. **How do you know that small kids were working like this?***
*8. **If you could choose which time would you live in?***

After having discussed all 8 hazardous work conditions, Mr. Shakespeare concluded the lesson with a brief explanation of capitalism in the United States and how profits and cheap labor is related to capitalism.

Areas of Strength:
Responding to student questions.

Suggestions for Improvement and/or Growth:
1. Provide assignment (i.e., journal entry, do now, etc) during down time (announcements and breakfast).
2. Write a complete objective that is measureable (*please refer to grade level notes and handouts on writing complete objectives, also reference materials provided to you during our workshop on writing objectives.*)
3. Review lesson objective prior to beginning the lesson.
4. Differentiate assignments based on student need/interest.
5. Utilize technology as instructional tool (*overhead projector*)
6. Minimize the amount of time that students spend on transferring writings from one sheet of paper to another (back of assignment paper to lined paper).
7. Activate prior knowledge prior to starting new lesson or introducing new concepts.
8. Provide background knowledge prior to the lesson.
9. Adhere to balanced literacy format.
10. Use lesson opener (read aloud).
11. Adhere to district and school policy on entering student attendance daily, updating Progressive Writing Wall, Utilization of Cell Phone during instructional time, updating bulletin board/posting student work.

Suggested Resources for Improvement

Books
1. The Content-Rich Reading and Writing Workshop by *Nancy Akhavan*

2. Using Picture Books in Middle School Grades 6-8 by *Teacher Created Materials, Inc*.
3. Beyond Words: Picture Books for Older Readers and Writers
4. Improving Comprehension with Think-Aloud Strategies: Modeling What Good Readers Do by *Jeffrey D. Wilhem, Ph.D*.
5. Classroom Instruction That Works: Research Based Strategies for Increasing Student Achievement by Marzano, *Pickering and Pollock*.
6. Differentiating Instruction in the Regular Classroom by *Diane Heacox, Ed.D,*

Research Reports/Articles

- Seven Literacy Strategies That Work by Douglas Fisher, Nancy Frey and Douglas Williams (*article attached*)

LESSON SUMMARY

Objective (as written on the board):
Students will talk about ways to show respect for others
Students will be able to develop an understanding of the School District Policy on harassment and bullying.

Summary:
On the day of the observation there were twenty-eight students present. As students entered the classroom they were assigned seats. Mr. Powell launched the lesson with a discussion on respect. After the initial discussion on respect Mr. Powell showed a film about respect and bias. Once during the movie, Mr. Powell stopped to have a brief discussion with students of a scenario presented in the movie; he then started the movie again. At the end of the movie, Mr. Powell reviewed the key areas covered in the movie. Mr. Powell then handed out index cards to the students and asked them to write a nice note to someone using "put up" words. After completing their notes, students shared their notes with their peers. Mr. Powell closed the lesson with assigning students homework.

SUGGESTIONS FOR IMPROVEMENT/GROWTH
- Align lesson objectives with State Standards (include standard on the board next to objective)
- Review lesson objective with students prior to the lesson
- Arrange desks in a configuration that is conducive to your lesson. For example, desks should have been arranged in a "U" shape to maximize student to student and teacher to student engagement
- Post more student work
- Post Crisis Room/ISS rules and consequences
- Review lesson plan/notes prior to the lesson, do not use notes as a script for the entire lesson.
- Use scaffolding techniques when working with students; help them to work out the answers, do not give them the answers directly.
- Put up interactive progressive word wall
- Review all of the vocabulary words prior to engaging in the lesson
- Create a schedule outlining activities for the day (conflict mediation, student reflection, independent class work time, lunch, etc.)

Recommended Books
- Using-Peer-Mediation-in-Classrooms-and-Schools, James Gilhooley
- Student-Resolving-Conflict, Richard-Cohen

LESSON SUMMARY

Objective (as written on the board):

There was no objective written on the board

Summary:
On the day of the planned observation Ms. Diva did not have her scheduled students present. The students were present in school but were not picked up. Ms. Diva was updating her bulletin boards and student folders.

Suggestions for Improvement and/or Growth:
- Provide services to students according to your approved schedule
- Do not cancel classes without prior administrator approval
- Write complete objectives daily
- Communicate with administration when you are experiencing difficultly

LESSON SUMMARY

Objective (as written on the board):
STUDENT WILL BE ABLE TO investigate place value.
STUDENT WILL BE ABLE TO investigate decimals with adding and subtracting

Summary:
On the day of this observation there were thirty-five students present. The lesson began with the math message which was projected on to a screen in front of the classroom:

What is the value of the number that's underlined:

(1)832266	(2) 598449
(3)19883	(4) 64544
(5) 66.162	(6) 94932
(7) 81.86	(8) 9.271
(9) 36212	(10) 706.2

As students worked independently to complete the math box, Ms. Jones distributed decimal place value sheets (downloaded from www.math-drills). Additionally, Ms. Jones directed the students to turn to page 396 in their reference book. Ms. Jones called on students randomly to provide answers to the questions that were on the overhead. As students provided the teacher with the correct answer, they were rewarded with a treat (candy). Students who demonstrated difficulty in solving the problem were provided assistance by one of their peers. When students shared their answers, Ms. Jones challenged the class to question the accuracy of the answers their peers provided. After all ten problems had been reviewed, Ms. Jones transitioned the students into a hands on place value activity requiring the use of base 10 blocks. Ms. Jones provided the students with two-three digit numbers to demonstrate their understanding of place value by utilizing the base 10 blocks (432 and 698). When students completed their base 10 block arrangements, Ms. Jones modeled solving the problem by drawing the base 10 blocks on the overhead. All students received a sticker for getting the problems correct. After reviewing the second number, the students were informed that they would be working in pairs. Students cleared the base 10 blocks and were given large poster paper and markers. Ms. Jones provided the class with additional problems and they were given six minutes to complete them. At the end of the six minutes, students presented their answers to their peers. At the end of the lesson students were given their homework assignment.

Areas of Strength:

Rapport with Students—Ms. Jones respects individual differences in the temperament and learning preferences of the students without compromising classroom objectives. She provides corrections for incorrect responses in a manner conducive to maintaining positive self-esteem in her students. Ms. Jones has demonstrated the ability to establish effective intervention techniques with her students.

Providing Feedback to students/Clarity of Presentation—Ms. Jones enhances student understanding through the use of appropriate resources and supplemental materials (overhead, handouts and manipulatives).

Suggestions for Improvement and/or Growth:
Planning
- Adhere to the EveryDay Math Curriculum lesson components
- Align STATE STANDARDS to daily objectives (including CPIs).
- Include differentiated instructional activities for students per IEPs
- Adhere to district pacing when planning lessons
- Attach sample of higher order questions with lesson plan

Instruction
- Adhere to required lesson components
- Ask higher order questions that will require students to apply and synthesize the content that you are presenting.
- Additionally, it is recommended that Ms. Jones attend the 5th Grade level meetings to receive on-going support in completing lesson plans and improved pedagogical strategies.
- Ms. Jones should also spend more time with the Math Coach to discuss district pacing and the appropriate amount of time to spend on individual skills.

Suggested Readings
- What Every Teacher Should Know about Instructional Planning, by Tileston
- Effective Instruction for Students with Special Needs by Algozzine and Ysseldyke
- Differentiating Math Instruction Strategies that work for K-8 Classroom

Suggested Websites
- National Council of Teachers of Math: www.nctm.org
- Writing Plans from the Teachers Desk: www.teachersdesk.org

FORMATIVE TEACHER OBSERVATION #5

7th Grade Class
Math (Inclusion)

LESSON SUMMARY

OBJECTIVE:

The learner will write an algorithm for partial products by solving 5 partial products problems.
(OBJECTIVE NOT THE SAME THAT WAS DISCUSSED DURING THE PRE OBSERVATION CONFERENCE—OBJECTIVE IS NOT THE OBJECTIVE INDICATED ON THE LESSON PLAN FOR THIS LESSON)

SUMMARY:

On the day of the observation there were 39 students present. Students were arranged in four cooperative groups. As Ms. Janee, the lead teacher presented the lesson, Ms. Bonet inclusion teacher, circulated around the classroom to provide varied levels of support. Students entered the classroom and immediately reported to their assigned seats. Students began working on the Do Now that was written on the board

Write a number sentence 3.7*6.2 and 1.2*2.7

As students worked on completing the do now, Ms. Janee reminded the students that they should not be multiplying but estimating, you will need decimal points in the answer. Also written on the board was the days' activities: Do Now, Rounding vs Magnitude Estimates, MJ 47, MM 53, Partial Products, SRB 19, MJ 50-51, MM 56, Game/MJ 52/53, Summary and Homework. After approximately 5-7 minutes, Ms. Janee went to the white board to model solving the Do Now problem. Ms. Janee then transitioned the students into the lesson on rounding and estimating. Students were asked to write down the steps for rounding in their notebooks. After reviewing the strategies students were given problems to complete independently. Students were given five minutes to complete the problems with reminders by Ms. Janee that they were expected to apply the strategies previously presented. As students worked to complete their problems, Ms. Janee went to each set of cooperatively grouped students to gauge their progress. As Ms. Janee reviewed students' answers, she reminded students to estimate to solve the problems and that they should not multiply. Ms. Janee went over the problems with the students as a class and then she assigned students a problem to complete on their own: 193.2*35. After reviewing the solution and strategies with the class, Ms. Janee assigned the students an assignment out of their workbook. At this time, Ms. Bonet worked with her group in a separate area in the classroom. As students worked on their assignment, students anxiously requested that Ms. Bonet review their answers. When students completed their work they were given additional work or were assigned to go the computer center. The lesson ended with Ms. Janee reviewing strategies for solving the problems. Ms. Janee distributed quizzes that students had taken earlier; she provided them with the opportunity to correct one of their problems using the strategies that were revisited during this lesson.

106

FORMATIVE TEACHER OBSERVATION #6

6/7 Special Needs
Language Arts

LESSON SUMMARY

Objective (as written on the board):
Identify and analyze figurative language devices in Sounder by completing organizers and charts categorizing figurative devices and how they relate to setting/mood and themes throughout the novel with 75-85% accuracy.

Summary:
On the day of the observation there were seventeen special needs students (BD) and three aides present. Dr. Angelou began the LAL lesson with a quick write.

Have you ever been treated unfairly? How did it make you feel?

She then transitioned into a Read Aloud—To Be A Slave. After the read aloud, students engaged in a comparative analysis discussion where they compared the characters and the setting from the novel To Be A Slave with characters and setting in Sounder. Students then engaged in a conversation about how African Americans were treated during the Slavery era and currently with the first African American President elect. After these two engaging discussions, the teacher transitioned the class into a review of vocabulary words from Chapter 2 of Sounder. Students were asked to review the words and then completed a crossword puzzle as a whole class activity. Students were asked to identify the vocabulary words according to the definitions provided. After the completion of the crossword puzzle, the teacher asked students to read from Chapter 2 of Sounder. After the students completed their readings, the teacher extracted two sentences from the reading, placed them on the overhead to discuss the sensory words in the sentences. Students were asked to identify and define the descriptive words in the sentences that had been projected onto the board. After discussing sentences and sections of the assigned chapter, students were then asked to assemble into assigned groups for center activities. One group was assigned to the computer center with an aide, another group was assigned to work on a small group activity with another aide and the third group worked with Dr. Angelou at the library center. The students working with Dr. Angelou continued reading Sounder, discussing various aspects of the chapter. After the center activities, students came back together as a whole class to work on their persuasive writing task. Prior to writing, Dr. Angelou engaged the class into a discussion on persuasive writing and the class discussed the various ways that they could persuade their parents to purchase items that they wished for Christmas. The lesson ended with the class completing a pros and cons graphic organizer related to their persuasive writing task.

Areas of Strength:
Planning balanced literacy lesson differentiating activities based on student needs
Seamless transition from activity to activity

Suggestions for Improvement and/or Growth:
Round Robin reading is not appropriate during whole group instruction. Students should be encouraged to read at the instructional level **ONLY** during guided reading in small groups.

Suggested Readings
ARTICLE ON ROUND ROBIN READING -Attached

LESSON SUMMARY

Objective:
As written on the board
- To find areas of polygons drawn on a grid
- Enclose a rectangle subtract unwanted parts

Written on Scroll Chart on the Black Board
As written on the board
- Objectives
- 5th To factor numbers
- 6th To find experimental probability
- To identify rotation reflections
- 8th To develop concept of square root

Summary:
On the day of the observation there were twenty-four students (6th and 8th Grade) present and two teachers, Ms. Espanola's and Mr. Tane. The lesson was delayed fifteen minutes due to Ms. Espanola's failure to pick up the students from their classes as required. After reporting to the classroom, the students were asked to sit in the back at five tables (cooperative group). Ms. Espanola began the lesson by asking students to complete their Do Now (in English) which was located in their EveryDay Math Books (5th Grade Spanish version). Ms. Espanola spoke to the students in Spanish for the majority of the lesson observation, despite the fact that all of the students were not native Spanish speakers. Ms. Espanola spoke minimal English to the students during this lesson; more specifically one word responses. However, questions asked by the students in Spanish that required a more detailed response were spoken in Spanish by Ms. Espanola .

Areas for Improvement and/or Growth:
- Follow lesson plans and district pacing guide for Math
- Students should be given grade level instructional materials
- Encourage students to ask questions and to respond to you in English
- Provide instruction to students in English
- Attend weekly content (Math) meetings
- Arrange desks in cooperative groups
- Create learning centers that are inviting
- Post more student work
- Remove commercial posters from bulletin boards (place elsewhere in the classroom)

LESSON SUMMARY

Objective (as written on the board):
By the end of the lesson, **STUDENT WILL BE ABLE TO** explore basic probability concepts such as fair game, experimental probability, theoretical probability and fraction rotation

Summary:
On the day of this observation there were thirty-seven students present. The lesson began with the do now written on the board.

Due Now (as written on the board)
(1)2/4   (2) 3/6
(3) 4/12   (4) 6/24
(5) 3/9   (6) 10/15
(7) 15/20   (8) 10/20

Students entered the classroom and went to their assigned seats. Ms. Hyperbole directed them to get their books and to begin working on the do now on the board. Ms. Hyperbole gave the students five minutes to complete the problems and she informed them that they would be going to the board to write their answers. Students went to the board to record their answers. All answers were discussed with the students in the class, specifically strategies. After reviewing the last problem Ms. Hyperbole shared with the students a strategy on solving problems with zeroes (ie 100/500). Steve was asked by Ms. Hyperbole to distribute blocks to each group of students. Students were directed to the problem written on the board. Students were asked to write the problem down in their notebooks.

Foot Locker has 12 Jordan sneakers. Each pair comes in different colors. Their are equally likely to be bought. Find the probability. (as written on the board)

Ms. Hyperbole asked students to define probability from their notes. After reading and discussing probability, Ms. Hyperbole demonstrated probability by tossing a coin several times. After discussing the probability of heads and tales, Ms. Hyperbole transitioned the students to the assignment on the board. Students were asked to take out three blue blocks, 3 yellow blocks and 6 red blocks. Ms. Hyperbole then asked students to count the number of sneakers based on the blocks they had sorted (each block represented one sneaker). Students were then asked to find the probability of someone purchasing a red sneaker, a yellow sneaker and a blue sneaker. The class ended with a summary of probability and students were permitted to begin working on their homework assignment (5 minutes remained in the lesson).

Areas of Strength:

Rapport with Students—Ms. Hyperbole respects individual differences in the temperament and learning preferences of the students without compromising classroom objectives. She provides corrections for incorrect responses in a manner conducive to maintaining positive self-esteem in her students. Ms. Hyperbole has demonstrated the ability to establish effective intervention techniques with her students.

Providing Feedback to students/Clarity of Presentation—Ms. Hyperbole enhances student understanding through the use of appropriate resources and supplemental materials (overhead, handouts and manipulatives).

Lesson Planning—great improvement in planning lessons according to Connected Math and EveryDay Math guidelines as well in the development of specific, measureable lesson objectives

Suggestions for Improvement and/or Growth:
Planning

- Review text on board for errors.
- Hand students treats as opposed to throwing treats at them
- Ask higher order questions
- Continue open communication and dialogue with teachers and the child study team in reference to student progress or challenges.

FORMATIVE TEACHER OBSERVATION #9

6th/7th Grade Special Needs
Math

LESSON SUMMARY

Objective: (As written on the board)
No Objective was Written on the Board

Summary:
The Connected Math period began with students waiting for breakfast to be delivered by breakfast monitors. The breakfast monitors arrived to the classroom at 8:40am, breakfast was distributed and students ate their breakfast. At approximately 8:50am, Mr. Egypt announced to the class that they had five minutes to complete their breakfast. As each student finished their breakfast, Mr. Egypt handed students a Multiplication Lattice Worksheet downloaded from the Free Mathsheet Worksheets at www.math.drill.com. One student (Tim) was unsure about what he was expected to do with the worksheet and he asked Mr. Egypt for clarification. In responding to the student request for information about the worksheet, Mr. Egypt informed the class that they should complete the lattice side of the worksheet first and that the worksheet was a warm-up. After the explanation, another student asked Mr. Egypt if the worksheet was a test. Mr. Egypt provided assistance to students who were struggling with completing the problems on the worksheet. At approximately 9:10am, Mr. Egypt went to the board and wrote the following:

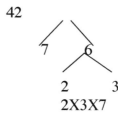

Mr. Egypt wrote the problems from the worksheet on the board and called on one student Lisa very frequently to provide an explanation of the strategy used to solve the problems. At 9:20am, Mr. Egypt instructed the student to line up for their activity.

Suggestions for Improvement and/or Growth:

- Write the objective and corresponding STATE STANDARDS and CPI on the board for each lesson taught.
- Begin each lesson with a review of the lesson objective, STATE STANDARDS and CPI.

- Implement Connected Math Curriculum as required.
- Integrate breakfast with mini lesson/Do Now/Reinforcement Activity (instructional breakfast).
- Assign classroom aide to pick up breakfast so that breakfast is not late.
- Adhere to lesson as indicated on approved lesson plan.
- Meet with Math Coach for assistance in implementing district Math Curriculum.
- Establish Centers, particularly Math Centers that support Connected Math.
- Update student work
- Utilize instructional support materials provided in the Connected Math Curriculum
- Discontinue using unapproved "dittos."

Suggested Websites
- Connected Math Website

LESSON SUMMARY

Objective (as written on the board):

Summary:
On the day of the observation there were 38 students present. Mr. Dicey launched the lesson with a review of triangles (equilateral and isosceles). Mr. Dicey then transitioned the students into several activities which encouraged students to explore a variety of triangles; Prior to students working in their assigned groups on their problems, Mr. Dicey went to the board to model completing a problem. Students were then asked to work together as teams. At the end of the lesson, Mr. Dicey asked teams to report out and their peers were asked to critique team responses and strategies. At the end of the critique, students were asked to review the lesson objective and to decide as a class if they had been successful in achieving the objective of the lesson.

Areas of Strength:
Engaging students
Achieving instructional objectives

Suggestions for Improvement and/or Growth:
Continue to ask higher order questions
Include degree of mastery in lesson objective
Obtain additional books for classroom library (see Literacy Coach and Media Specialist)
Utilize scoring rubric during the summary (reporting out by students) of the lesson.

Suggested Readings
Designing and Assessing Educational Objectives: Applying Bloom's New Taxonomy

Domain II: The Classroom Environment E=Evident, NE=Not Evident,	E	NE	Not Observed
Creating an Environment of Respect and Rapport	X		
Teacher-student interactions are respectful	X		
Student-Student interactions are respectful			Na
Teacher-teacher interactions are respectful			
Managing Student Behavior		X	
Classroom rules and consequences posted		X	
Appropriate and timely response to student misbehavior		X	
Pillars of Character Education reinforced			
Managing Classroom Procedures		X	
Classroom jobs posted/rotated regularly		X	
Bathroom log evident		X	
Hall passes available and utilized		X	
Computer logs, procedures, rules and schedules evident.		X	
Library log evident.	X		
Supervision of volunteers and paraprofessionals	X		
Management of transitioning to-and-from classes.			X
Performance of non-instructional duties (posted and ancillary meetings)			X
Lunch time procedures followed			X
Timely dissemination of dated materials	X		
Classroom is orderly and well managed.			
Establishing a Culture for Learning			X
Students are involved in planning personal short and long term goals.		X	
Teacher communicated the importance and connection of content.	X		
Students demonstrate pride in their work.		X	
High teacher expectations are demonstrated.		X	
Student work is posted with a rubric and evidence of pride work is present.		X	
Content based word walls are interactive and progressive.		X	
Evidence of bulletin board guidelines		X	
Learning pods/cooperative groups		X	
Classroom resources are easily accessible		X	
Library area organized by genres and/or levels		X	
Evidence of EveryDay Math and daily routines posted		X	
Hallway bulletin board display current work.		X	
Computer centers maintained.			X
Science modules present in classroom and being used.		X	
Classroom Library (300) Reference Center			
Organizing Physical Space	X		
Clear and uncluttered pathways			

115

	E	NE	NA
Communicating Clearly and Accurately			
Use of content related vocabulary	X		
Directions and procedures are communicated clearly and accurately	X		
Oral and written language is clear and accurate	X		
Clearly communicates what is being taught	X		
Using questioning and Discussion Techniques		X	
Student use of higher order questioning and critical thinking techniques		X	
Students engaged in classroom discussions and debates		X	
Student discussions of specific strategies to be utilized		X	
Student articulation of objectives taught		X	
Flexible Guided Reading groups evident		X	
Engaging Students in Learning		X	
Differentiated activities	X		
Time-on-Task			X
Technology used appropriately			X
Grade appropriate manipulatives/calculators		X	
Evidence that science modules are being used	X		
Student engagement is 100%			X
Evidence of writing journals	X		
Evidence of district content initiatives in use			
Providing Feedback to Student	X		
Evidence of personal conferences	X		
Meaningful feedback provided on student work			X
Lesson adjustments are made according to need			
Feedback to students in a timely and consistent manner	X		
Attaining Student Achievement That Meets or Exceeds Performance Benchmarks	X		
Team teaching strategies are used effectively	X		
Evidence of lesson alignment to the objective	X		
Evidence of teacher modeling and use of exemplars	X		
Student independent work is aligned to the objective	X		
Students are able to apply learned content to independent work	X		

INFORMAL FEEDBACK SUMMARY

Students were working on quiz and then completed a lab sheet.
Teacher provided support and encouragement to students as she walked around.

Both teachers walked around the classroom to provide assistance to the students as they completed their assignment.

WHERE ARE THE SCIENCE MODULES???? THEY SHOULD BE VISIBLE AND LABELED.

INFORMAL OBSERVATION FORM

Domain II Classroom Environment
E = Evident , NE = Not-Evident, NO= Not Observed, NA = Not Applicable

Creating an Environment of Respect and Rapport

E	NE	NO	NA	
☑	☐	☐	☐	Teacher-student interactions are respectful
☑	☐	☐	☐	Student- Student interactions are respectful
☐	☐	☐	☑	Teacher-teacher interactions are respectful

Managing Student Behavior

E	NE	NO	NA	
☐	☑	☐	☐	Classroom rules and consequences posted
☑	☐	☐	☐	Appropriate and timely response to student misbehavior
☐	☐	☐	☐	Pillars of Character Education reinforced

Managing Classroom Procedures

E	NE	NO	NA	
☐	☑	☐	☐	Classroom jobs posted/ rotated regularly
☐	☑	☐	☐	Bathroom log evident
☐	☐	☐	☑	Hall passes available and utilized
☐	☑	☐	☐	Computer logs, procedures, rules and schedules evident
☐	☑	☐	☐	Library log evident
☐	☐	☐	☑	Supervision of volunteers and paraprofessionals
☐	☐	☑	☐	Management of transitioning to- and- from classes
☐	☐	☑	☐	Performance of non-instructional duties (post and ancillary meetings)
☐	☐	☑	☐	Lunch time procedures followed
☐	☐	☑	☐	Timely dissemination of dated materials
☑	☐	☐	☐	Classroom is orderly and well managed

Establishing a Culture for Learning

E	NE	NO	NA	
☐	☐	☑	☐	Students are involved in planning personal short and long term goals
☐	☐	☐	☐	Teacher communicate the importance and connection of content
☐	☐	☐	☐	Students demonstrate pride in their work
☑	☐	☐	☐	High teacher expectations are demonstrated
☑	☐	☐	☐	Student work is posted with a rubric and evidence of pride in work is present
☑	☐	☐	☐	Content based word walls are interactive and progressive
☐	☐	☐	☐	Evidence of bulletin board guidelines
☑	☐	☐	☐	Learning pods/cooperative groups
☑	☐	☐	☐	Classroom resources are easily accessible
☐	☑	☐	☐	Library area organized by genres and/or levels
☐	☐	☐	☑	Evidence of Everyday Math and daily routines posted
☐	☑	☐	☐	Hallway bulletin board display current work
☑	☐	☐	☐	Computer centers maintained
☑	☐	☐	☐	Science modules present in classroom and being used
☐	☑	☐	☐	Classroom Library (300 books) Reference Center

INFORMAL OBSERVATION FORM

Domain II Classroom Environment

E = Evident , NE = Not-Evident, NO= Not Observed, NA = Not Applicable

Creating an Environment of Respect and Rapport

E	NE	NO	NA	
				Teacher-student interactions are respectful
☑	☐	☐	☐	Student- Student interactions are respectful
☑	☐	☐	☐	Teacher-teacher interactions are respectful
☐	☐	☐	☑	

Managing Student Behavior

E	NE	NO	NA	
				Classroom rules and consequences posted
☑	☐	☐	☐	Appropriate and timely response to student misbehavior
☑	☐	☐	☐	Pillars of Character Education reinforced
☑	☐	☐	☐	

Managing Classroom Procedures

E	NE	NO	NA	
				Classroom jobs posted/ rotated regularly
☐	☑	☐	☐	Bathroom log evident
☐	☑	☐	☐	Hall passes available and utilized
☑	☐	☐	☐	Computer logs, procedures, rules and schedules evident
☐	☑	☐	☐	Library log evident
☐	☑	☐	☐	Supervision of volunteers and paraprofessionals
☐	☐	☐	☑	Management of transitioning to- and- from classes
☐	☐	☑	☐	Performance of non-instructional duties (post and ancillary meetings)
☐	☐	☑	☐	Lunch time procedures followed
☐	☐	☑	☐	Timely dissemination of dated materials
☐	☐	☑	☐	Classroom is orderly and well managed
☑	☐	☐	☐	

Establishing a Culture for Learning

E	NE	NO	NA	
				Students are involved in planning personal short and long term goals
☐	☐	☑	☐	Teacher communicate the importance and connection of content
☑	☐	☐	☐	Students demonstrate pride in their work
☑	☐	☐	☐	High teacher expectations are demonstrated
☑	☐	☐	☐	Student work is posted with a rubric and evidence of pride in work is present
☐	☑	☐	☐	Content based word walls are interactive and progressive
☐	☑	☐	☐	Evidence of bulletin board guidelines
☐	☑	☐	☐	Learning pods/cooperative groups
☐	☑	☐	☐	Classroom resources are easily accessible
☐	☑	☐	☐	Library area organized by genres and/or levels
☐	☑	☐	☐	Evidence of Everyday Math and daily routines posted
☐	☐	☐	☑	Hallway bulletin board display current work
☐	☑	☐	☐	Computer centers maintained
☑	☐	☐	☐	Science modules present in classroom and being used
☑	☐	☐	☐	

7th Grade
Social Studies

Enduring Understanding: How and why do societies change? What is civilization and how has it been defined? Why do civilizations decline and perish? Why is there political and social conflict? How does religion influence the development of individual societies as well as global processes?

Objective: The learner will learn about the influence of Islam in the fields of Science, Geography , Medicine, Mathematics, Philosophy and other areas of modern society and culture. The learner will understand the importance of Muslim civilization in mediating long-distance commercial, cultural, intellectual, and food crop exchange across Eurasia and parts of Africa . The student will see the significance of the lasting contributions made to the progress of civilization by Arabic and Islamic societies.

Selected Text: Holt World History, Video History's Impact

Essential Questions: Why do we study history? What do we know about Islam from our present day historical context? What were the contributions made by the Arabic world to Geography, science, mathematics, medicine, literature, and philosophy?

	Monday	Tuesday	Wednesday	Thursday	Friday
Assessment	Lesson Summary	Written response identifying the significance of one Arabic contribution to medicine.	Worksheet response to Arabic poetry and literature.	New Vocabulary terms used in summary response.	
Materials	HOLT World History, Note books, hand out, pencils.	HOLT World History, Note books, hand out, pencils.	HOLT World History, Note books, hand out, pencils.	HOLT World History, Note books, hand out, pencils.	HOLT World History, Note books, hand out, pencils.
Time period	45 Minutes	45 minutes	45 minutes	45 minute period	45 minute period

Accommodations	Charting information from the text and Discussion.	Groups working together to review first and secondary sources.	Students will work in groups to create a presentation explaining one Arabic contribution to science.	Students will work collectively and individually to benefit from the sharing of ideas and verbally expressing their understanding.	Class discussion of new vocabulary words, and drafting of sentences that demonstrate meaning in context.
Procedures	We will discuss the influence of Islam on the Arabic culture and the respect and tolerance of Islam for other cultures and religions. We will discuss various significant contributions of the Arabic world to civilization and modern medicine, science, and mathematics..	We will engage in reviewing Arabic Philosophy and poetry by analyzing primary sources of literature, poetry and philosophy. We will read and discuss texts in group	We will collectively view and discuss the students' main arguments and critiques about the story. We will create outlines that help students organize their ideas and prepare for a revision of their drafts.	We will have individual writing time combined with collaborative group discussion so students can share their ideas and make suggestions to fellow students' writings.	We will collectively define and utilize new words in context, reviewing their meaning and usage.
HW	Students will write a reflection on the days lesson and discussion.	Today we discussed various contributions of the Arabic world the students will write a response on how one contribution has bettered our world.	Students will write a response to the philosophical ideas expressed in Kahlih Gibrand's *The Prophet* .	Students will write brief explanations in their own words of new vocabulary terms.	

119

5ᵗʰ Grade LAL

UNIT THEME: LOOK INSIDE- Elena

Essential Questions: How do readers construct meaning from text? How do I figure out a word I do not know? How do good writers express themselves? How does process shape the writing product? How are present events related to past events?

Enduring Understanding:- Good readers employ strategies to help them understand text. Strategic readers can develop, select, and apply strategies to enhance their comprehension. Good readers compare, infer, synthesize, and make connections (text to text, text to world, text to self) to make text personally relevant and useful Rules, conventions of language, help readers understand what is being communicated. Good writers develop and refine their ideas for thinking, learning, communicating, and aesthetic expression. Good writers use a repertoire of strategies that enables them to vary form and style, in order to write for different purposes, audiences, and contexts. There are varying perspectives on the meaning of historical events.

	DAY 6 MONDAY	DAY 7 TUESDAY
Objectives	1) After creating 5 questions from Elena and narrative elements, the learner will analyze and extract information from the text by identifying and defending their response to each of the 5 questions 2) After receiving their story back and a review of the class ending the learner will examine the body of their essay and create an ending by writing at least 5 sentences to their ending of their essay.	1) After reviewing the key components of writing an essay from the class written essay, learner will be able to understand all of the key components of writing an essay by writing and publishing a 4 to 5 paragraph essay.
ASSESSMENTS	review game, vocabulary game, closing	Multiple choice Comprehension test, Vocabulary test, opened responses, ending of essay
MATERIALS	Pens, paper, pencils, overhead projector, text, computers, etc.	Pens, paper, pencils, overhead projector, text, computers, etc.
PROCEDURES Oral Language Sharing Literature Group Inclusion: Literature Read Aloud, Journal Sharing, Journal Writing- with Whole Class	Readers Workshop Journal Writing If you were in the story, what would you have done if the soldiers were approaching your home?	READER WORKSHOP Reading Test being administered HARCOURT READING ASSESSMENT FOR ELENA
SKILLS AND STRATEGIES 15-20 minutes -Comprehension and Vocabulary	Reading Skill Review Narrative Elements *inclusion: using T5-alternative teaching strategies: focus, reteach the skill, summarize and assess	Group Inclusion: testing in separate classroom environment, additional time will be provided Questions and answer choices will be read aloud to students Test will be given in page by page
READING 30-45 Minutes	Guided Reading Think and Respond Questions, pg128	

-Guided and Independent	*inclusion students will be assisted in answering think and respond. Students will be provided with R.A.C.E.R to reinforce usage in answering the questions **BALL GAME REVIEW** -review the story using the ball game (Students will ask each other questions about the story and when they do not know the answer they have to redirect the question to another student for the answer; this process is ongoing and the teacher is facilitating the activity. Students must come up with at least 3 questions of their own to ask other students) * inclusion students must come up with 2 questions- **Vocabulary Review Game** (Students pick an egg which contains a vocabulary word and in groups, students have to act out the meaning of the word while the other groups have to guess the word and write it on a white board) *inclusion students will complete with whole-class and mainstreamed **Question of the Day** If you were in the story, what would you have done if the soldiers were approaching your home?	
LANGUAGE ARTS 45-90 MINTUES **Writing** -Research Paper Prompts will be visual to the student either on the project or poster paper The students will use the rubric every day in writing making sure they are following the criteria for each area	**WRITERS WORKSHOP** **Writing** Teacher/student review the ending of the class essay. Students will receive an essay and have to compose an ending for the essay. Teacher conference while students are working on their essay. Student/Student proof read each others while waiting on the teacher **Group Inclusion:** Teacher will work with students in small group on a strong closing to an essay. Group will independently complete an ending for the class essay after teacher modeling **Grammar:** Review compound subject and compound predicate **Daily Language Practice** 1)i cannot believe it I screamed at the top of my lungs 2)why is this happening to me	**WRITERS WORKSHOP** **Writing** Teacher/student review the ending of the class essay. Stress details Students will receive their original essay and publish it. Teacher will conference while students are writing. Student/student proof read while teacher is conferencing. **Group Inclusion:** Teacher will work with students in small group on a strong closing to an essay. Group will independently complete an ending for the class essay after teacher modeling **Grammar:** Review compound subject and compound predicate *inclusion students with whole-class

Spelling Words Placed on interactive wall in front of class	Treasure, capture, feature, pleasure, measure, creature, picture, adventure, mixture, structure, pasture, culture, literature, furniture, temperature, legislature, immature, leisure, premature, signature **Modified Spelling List for Inclusion students-15 words instead of 20; taken from Dolch sight word list-to increase the sight of these high frequency words and for usage in writing**	Treasure, capture, feature, pleasure, measure, creature, picture, adventure, mixture, structure, pasture, culture, literature, furniture, temperature, legislature, immature, leisure, premature, signature **Modified Spelling List for Inclusion students-15 words instead of 20; taken from Dolch sight word list-to increase the sight of these high frequency words and for usage in writing**
HOMEWORK	Independent Reading & Writing activity; Grammar & Vocabulary Workbook nightly Exercises,	Independent Reading & Writing activity; Grammar & Vocabulary Workbook nightly Exercises
COMPUTER SCHEDULE	Students rotate on a class computer schedule and log into and work on the 5th Grade Harcourt Website for the story Elena.	Students rotate on a class computer schedule and log into and work on the 5th Grade Harcourt Website for the story Elena.

SUPPLEMENTARY RESOURCES
CHAPTER SEVEN
COMPETENCY SIX

Books

Wilmore, E. L. (2013). *Passing the Special Education TExES Exam.* Corwin Press.

Texas Public School Organization and Administration: 2012 [Misc. Supplies] VORNBERG JAMES A (Author), CONSILIENCE LLC (Author), BORGEMENKE ARTHUR J (Author)

Teacher Evaluation That Makes a Difference: A New Model for Teacher Growth and Student Achievement by Marzano, Robert J. and Toth, Michael D. (Jun 12, 2013)

Getting Teacher Evaluation Right: What Really Matters for Effectiveness and Improvement by Darling-Hammond, Linda (Jun 6, 2013)

Rethinking Teacher Supervision and Evaluation: How to Work Smart, Build Collaboration, and Close the Achievement... by Marshall, Kim (Mar 28, 2013)

The Framework for Teaching Evaluation Instrument, 2013 Edition: The newest rubric enhancing the links to the Common... by Charlotte Danielson (Jan 11, 2013)

Clinical Supervision and Teacher Development, 6th Edition by Gall, M. D. and Acheson, Keith A. (Sep 27, 2010)

Blandford, S. (2012). *Managing professional development in schools.* Routledge.

Articles

Calderhead, J. (2012). The contribution of research on teachers' thinking to the professional development of teachers. *Research on teacher thinking: understanding professional development. London*, 11-18.

Daley, G., & Kim, L. (2010). A Teacher Evaluation System That Works. Working Paper. *National Institute for Excellence in Teaching.*

Darling-Hammond, L., Amrein-Beardsley, A., Haertel, E., & Rothstein, J. (2012). Evaluating teacher evaluation. *Phi Delta Kappan, 93*(6), 8-15.

Fang, Z. (2013). Learning to Teach Against the Institutional Grain: A Professional Development Model for Teacher Empowerment. In *Preparing Teachers for the 21st Century* (pp. 237-250). Springer Berlin Heidelberg.

Gall, M. D., & Acheson, K. A. (2011). *Clinical supervision and teacher development*. John Wiley and Sons.

Hallinger, P., Heck, R. H., & Murphy, J. (2014). Teacher evaluation and school improvement: An analysis of the evidence. *Educational Assessment, Evaluation and Accountability*, 1-24.

Hanushek, E. A. (2011). The economic value of higher teacher quality. *Economics of Education Review*, *30*(3), 466-479.

Herlihy, C., Karger, E., Pollard, C., Hill, H. C., Kraft, M. A., Williams, M., & Howard, S. (2013). State and local efforts to investigate the validity and reliability of scores from teacher evaluation systems. *Teachers College Record*.

Koedel, C., & Betts, J. R. (2011). Does student sorting invalidate value-added models of teacher effectiveness? An extended analysis of the Rothstein critique. *Education*, *6*(1), 18-42.

Looney, J. (2011). Developing High-Quality Teachers: teacher evaluation for improvement. *European Journal of Education*, *46*(4), 440-455.

Nolan Jr, J., & Hoover, L. A. (2011). *Teacher supervision and evaluation*. John Wiley and Sons.

Taylor, E. S., & Tyler, J. H. (2012). Can Teacher Evaluation Improve Teaching. *Education Next*, *12*(4), 10.

Walsh, E., & Lipscomb, S. (2013). *Classroom Observations from Phase 2 of the Pennsylvania Teacher Evaluation Pilot: Assessing Internal Consistency, Score Variation, and Relationships with Value Added* (No. 7817). Mathematica Policy Research.

Webb, A. S. (2012). Teacher evaluation instruments: The processes and protocols in Washington State.

Websites and Blogs

https://www.authenticeducation.org/
http://www.schoolimprovement.com
http://www.tea.state.tx.us
http://www.corestandards.org

http://pdkintl.org/publications/kappan/
http://www.edweek.org/ew/index.html
http://www.naesp.org
http://learningforward.org/publications/learning-principal#.UxpZXxbog4M
http://www.wallacefoundation.org/Pages/default.aspx

Reports

Linking Teacher Evaluation to Professional Development: Focusing on Improving Teaching and Learning. Research & Policy Brief.
http://files.eric.ed.gov/fulltext/ED532775.pdf

Understanding by design. J McTighe
http://rt3region7.ncdpi.wikispaces.net/file/view/Intro+to+UBD+Handouts.pdf

UNDERSTANDING BY DESIGN® FRAMEWORK
J McTighe, G Wiggins
http://www.ascd.org/ASCD/pdf/siteASCD/publications/UbD_WhitePaper0312.pdf

" An Effective and Agonizing Way to Learn": Backwards Design and New Teachers' Preparation for Planning Curriculum.
N Graff
http://files.eric.ed.gov/fulltext/EJ940642.pdf

YouTube Videos

Making Teacher Evaluations Meaningful: Charlotte Danielson
Link
http://youtu.be/KzDcYuSsU2E
Embed
<iframe width="560" height="315" src="//www.youtube.com/embed/KzDcYuSsU2E" frameborder="0" allowfullscreen></iframe>

Teacher Evaluation Using The Danielson Framework
Link
http://youtu.be/5NDmaJoz2zw
Embed Code
<iframe width="420" height="315" src="//www.youtube.com/embed/5NDmaJoz2zw" frameborder="0" allowfullscreen></iframe>

Charlotte Danielson - Assessing Teacher Effectiveness
Link
http://youtu.be/86WKG_M0fgQ
Embed Code
<iframe width="420" height="315" src="//www.youtube.com/embed/86WKG_M0fgQ" frameborder="0" allowfullscreen></iframe>

Bill Gates: "How Do You Make a Teacher Great?" Part 1
Link

http://youtu.be/OnfzZEREfQs

Embed

<iframe width="420" height="315" src="//www.youtube.com/embed/OnfzZEREfQs" frameborder="0" allowfullscreen></iframe>

Dr. Robert Marzano Delivers Special Message To LCS Teachers (The Courage To Lead)
Link

http://youtu.be/4npJj4r1JDw

Embed

<iframe width="560" height="315" src="//www.youtube.com/embed/4npJj4r1JDw" frameborder="0" allowfullscreen></iframe>

Robert Marzano - 2012 School Administrators Conference
Link

http://youtu.be/clMRI8TX6Is

Embed

<iframe width="420" height="315" src="//www.youtube.com/embed/clMRI8TX6Is" frameborder="0" allowfullscreen></iframe>

Mini Projects/Additional Assignments

1. Review the teacher observations from the perspective of the Principal. Create staff develop plan for the Assistant Principals that conducted the observations.
2. Create a PowerPoint Presentation demonstrating how to make a good lesson better—you must select one of the lesson plans submitted with this case.
3. Create a PowerPoint Presentation demonstrating how to make a good lesson great you must use lesson observation presented in this case.
4. Create PowerPoint Presentation to present the staff development plan for the year. The audience will be the teachers.
5. Develop Agenda for Staff Development Session
6. Create Staff Development Workshop for the Teachers based on the data analyzed from this case.
7. Conduct comparative analysis of the Charlotte Danielson Teacher Observation Framework with the PDAS Observation Framework. Make recommendations on the framework that best suits the needs of the school.
8. Create a walkthrough schedule for two months which includes the areas that the observer will focus on (ie, higher questioning, teacher engagement, etc).
9. Create a walkthrough document that best meets the needs of your teachers.
10. Review each observation and provide suggestions for improvement. Draft a letter to each teacher outlining your recommendations—remember to include resources

that the teacher can use for reference in improving their pedagogy and lesson planning skills

Discussion/Reflection Topics

1. Teachers can change lives with just the right mix of chalk and challenges. **Joyce Meyer**

2. The single most important thing in a child's performance is the quality of the teacher. Making sure a child spends the maximum amount of time with inspirational teachers is the most important thing. **Michael Gove**

3. You can get help from teachers, but you are going to have to learn a lot by yourself, sitting alone in a room. **Dr. Seuss**

4. Most of us end up with no more than five or six people who remember us. Teachers have thousands of people who remember them for the rest of their lives. **Andy Rooney**

5. Education is the key to success in life, and teachers make a lasting impact in the lives of their students. **Solomon Ortiz**

6. Teachers are expected to reach unattainable goals with inadequate tools. The miracle is that at times they accomplish this impossible task. **Haim Ginott**

7. Everyone who remembers his own education remembers teachers, not methods and techniques. The teacher is the heart of the educational system. **Sidney Hook**

8. Education is a shared commitment between dedicated teachers, motivated students and enthusiastic parents with high expectations. **Bob Beauprez**

9. Police and firefighters are great, but they don't create wealth. They protect it. That's crucial. Teaching is a wonderful profession. Teachers help educate people to become good citizens so that citizens can then go create wealth. But they don't create the wealth themselves. **Rush Limbaugh**

10. The single most important thing in a child's performance is the quality of the teacher. Making sure a child spends the maximum amount of time with inspirational teachers is the most important thing. **Michael Gove**

CHAPTER 8
TeXes Principal Competency 7

(Photo Credit: U.S. Department of Agriculture (Flickr: 20120820-FNS-TRO-0005) [CC-BY-2.0 (http://creativecommons.org/licenses/by/2.0)], via Wikimedia Commons)

Strategic Independent School District
789372 Methodology Drive
Chess, TX 83982
www.sisd.edu
738-382-9302
738-382-3892 (Fax)

Dear Interim Principal,

I want to thank you for your willingness to serve as Interim Principal for the remainder of this school year. Albert Einstein Elementary School is in urgent need of immediate re-organization. The ability to think outside of the box will be required to satisfy the needs of the faculty, students and parents. There are several issues that have gone un-addressed that will need your immediate attention. I have attached for your perusal copies of letters from parents and teachers that will need creative strategizing to resolve. You will be pleased to know that there are competent staff members at Einstein who are willing to work collaboratively with you to get this building back on track. You are inheriting a young inexperienced staff who are enthusiastic about being at Einstein, they simply need a leader who is able to identify and match their strengths with the correct assignments.

Given the recent unexpected change in school leadership at Einstein, we are required to hold a community meeting to present to key school stakeholders our plan for the remainder of the school year. At this meeting, I will officially present you to the key school stakeholders and during this time you will be expected to present your immediate plans for re-organizing the building. My office will be in touch with you to provide you with the location and time of this event. Please do not hesitate to contact my office should you need assistance.

Sincerely Yours,

Dr. Aristotle Plato

Superintendent

Einstein Elementary School

Einstein Elementary School is located in a small rural town in East Texas. Einstein Elementary has had difficulty attracting and retaining school administrators and teachers. The community members of Chess are very committed to turning their elementary school around so that it can again be considered "Exemplary."

For this task, you will need to be creative in reorganizing the building. Remember the Texas principal knows how to apply organizational, decision-making, and problem solving skills to ensure an effective learning environment. Successfully re-organizing this building will demonstrate your understanding and mastery of:

Implement appropriate management techniques and group process skills to define roles, assign functions, delegate authority, and determine accountability for campus goal attainment.

Implement procedures for gathering, analyzing, and using data from a variety of sources for informed campus decision making.

Frame, analyze, and resolve problems using appropriate problem-solving techniques and decision-making skills.

Use strategies for promoting collaborative decision making and problem solving, facilitating team building, and developing consensus.

Encourage and facilitate positive change, enlist support for change, and overcome obstacles to change.

Apply skills for monitoring and evaluating change and making needed adjustments to achieve goals.

TEXAS EDUCATION AGENCY
Accountability Summary

Accountability Rating

Improvement Required

Met Standards on	Did Not Meet Standards on
- Student Progress	- Student Achievement
	- Closing Performance Gaps

Distinction Designation

Academic Achievement in Reading/ELA
Percent of Eligible Measures in Top Quartile 0 out of 4 = 0%
DOES NOT QUALIFY

Academic Achievement in Mathematics
Percent of Eligible Measures in Top Quartile 0 out of 3 = 0%
DOES NOT QUALIFY

Top 25 Percent Student Progress
DOES NOT QUALIFY

Performance Index Report

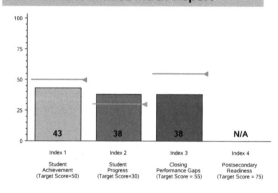

43	38	38	N/A
Index 1	Index 2	Index 3	Index 4
Student Achievement (Target Score=50)	Student Progress (Target Score=30)	Closing Performance Gaps (Target Score = 55)	Postsecondary Readiness (Target Score = 75)

Campus Demographics

Campus Type	Elementary
Campus Size	676 Students
Grade Span	EE - 05
Percent Economically Disadvantaged	98.2%
Percent English Language Learners	57.0%
Mobility Rate	20.3%

Performance Index Summary

Index	Points Earned	Maximum Points	Index Score
1 - Student Achievement	268	627	43
2 - Student Progress	537	1,400	38
3 - Closing Performance Gaps	230	600	38
4 - Postsecondary Readiness	N/A	N/A	N/A

System Safeguards

Number and Percent of Indicators Met

Performance Rates	5 out of 20 = 25%
Participation Rates	12 out of 12 = 100%
Graduation Rates	N/A
Total	**17 out of 32 = 53%**

TEXAS EDUCATION AGENCY
Student Achievement Data

	All Students	African American	Hispanic	White	American Indian	Asian	Pacific Islander	Two or More Races	Special Ed	Econ Disadv	ELL
STAAR Performance											
All Subjects											
Percent of Tests											
% at Phase-in 1 Level II or above	43%	39%	44%	40%	-	*	-	*	31%	42%	44%
% at Final Level II or above	14%	14%	14%	13%	-	*	-	*	17%	14%	15%
% at Level III Advanced	3%	3%	4%	0%	-	*	-	*	2%	3%	4%
Number of Tests											
# at Phase-in 1 Level II or above	268	56	203	6	-	*	-	*	27	254	130
# at Final Level II or above	88	20	66	2	-	*	-	*	15	82	45
# at Level III Advanced	21	4	17	0	-	*	-	*	2	19	11
Total Tests	627	144	461	15	-	*	-	*	86	607	293
Reading											
Percent of Tests											
% at Phase-in 1 Level II or above	43%	37%	44%	*	-	*	-	*	35%	42%	45%
% at Final Level II or above	15%	15%	15%	*	-	*	-	*	16%	14%	18%
% at Level III Advanced	4%	6%	4%	*	-	*	-	*	6%	4%	5%
Number of Tests											
# at Phase-in 1 Level II or above	96	20	71	*	-	*	-	*	11	90	44
# at Final Level II or above	33	8	24	*	-	*	-	*	5	30	18
# at Level III Advanced	9	3	6	*	-	*	-	*	2	8	5
Total Tests	222	54	160	*	-	*	-	*	31	214	98
Mathematics											
Percent of Tests											
% at Phase-in 1 Level II or above	50%	41%	56%	*	-	*	-	*	32%	50%	57%
% at Final Level II or above	16%	15%	18%	*	-	*	-	*	26%	16%	17%
% at Level III Advanced	5%	2%	6%	*	-	*	-	*	0%	5%	6%
Number of Tests											
# at Phase-in 1 Level II or above	112	22	89	*	-	*	-	*	10	106	56
# at Final Level II or above	36	8	28	*	-	*	-	*	8	34	17
# at Level III Advanced	11	1	10	*	-	*	-	*	0	10	6
Total Tests	222	54	160	*	-	*	-	*	31	214	98
Writing											
Percent of Tests											
% at Phase-in 1 Level II or above	18%	**	12%	*	-	-	-	-	*	18%	11%
% at Final Level II or above	4%	**	3%	*	-	-	-	-	*	4%	2%
% at Level III Advanced	0%	**	0%	*	-	-	-	-	*	0%	0%
Number of Tests											
# at Phase-in 1 Level II or above	16	**	8	*	-	-	-	-	*	16	5
# at Final Level II or above	4	**	2	*	-	-	-	-	*	4	1
# at Level III Advanced	0	**	0	*	-	-	-	-	*	0	0
Total Tests	91	**	66	*	-	-	-	-	*	90	47

131

	General Fund	%	Per Student	All Funds	%	Per Student
Expenditures by Object (Objects 6100-6600)						
Total Expenditures	4,353,255	100.00	5,401	5,146,570	100.00	6,385
Operating-Payroll	4,001,074	91.91	4,964	4,513,324	87.70	5,600
Other Operating	350,069	8.04	434	631,134	12.26	783
Non-Operating(Equipt/Supplies)	2,112	0.05	3	2,112	0.04	3
Expenditures by Function (Objects 6100-6400 Only)						
Total Operating Expenditures	4,351,143	100.00	5,398	5,144,458	100.00	6,383
Instruction (11,95) *	3,284,625	75.49	4,075	3,734,704	72.60	4,634
Instructional Res/Media (12) *	90,427	2.08	112	90,482	1.76	112
Curriculum/Staff Develop (13) *	47,743	1.10	59	72,290	1.41	90
Instructional Leadership (21) *	79,277	1.82	98	80,100	1.56	99
School Leadership (23) *	281,567	6.47	349	283,623	5.51	352
Guidance/Counseling Svcs (31) *	163,145	3.75	202	163,145	3.17	202
Social Work Services (32) *	7,157	0.16	9	7,157	0.14	9
Health Services (33) *	82,563	1.90	102	82,563	1.60	102
Food (35) **	0	0.00	0	302,829	5.89	376
Extracurricular (36) *	0	0.00	0	0	0.00	0
Plant Maint/Operation (51) * **	314,639	7.23	390	327,565	6.37	406
Security/Monitoring (52) * **	0	0.00	0	0	0.00	0
Data Processing Svcs (53)* **	0	0.00	0	0	0.00	0
Program expenditures by Program (Objects 6100-6400 only)						
Total Operating Expenditures	3,892,349	100.00	4,829	4,369,854	100.00	5,422
Regular	3,161,231	81.22	3,922	3,161,681	72.35	3,923
Gifted & Talented	87,640	2.25	109	87,640	2.01	109
Career & Technical	0	0.00	0	0	0.00	0
Students with Disabilities	327,160	8.41	406	458,111	10.48	568
Accelerated Education	1,058	0.03	1	130,580	2.99	162
Bilingual	147,815	3.80	183	150,158	3.44	186
Nondisc Alted-AEP Basic Serv	0	0.00	0	0	0.00	0
Disc Alted-DAEP Basic Serv	0	0.00	0	0	0.00	0
Disc Alted-DAEP Supplemental	0	0.00	0	0	0.00	0
T1 A Schoolwide-St Comp >=40%	167,445	4.30	208	381,684	8.73	474
Athletic Programming	0	0.00	0	0	0.00	0
High School Allotment	0	0.00	0	0	0.00	0

*

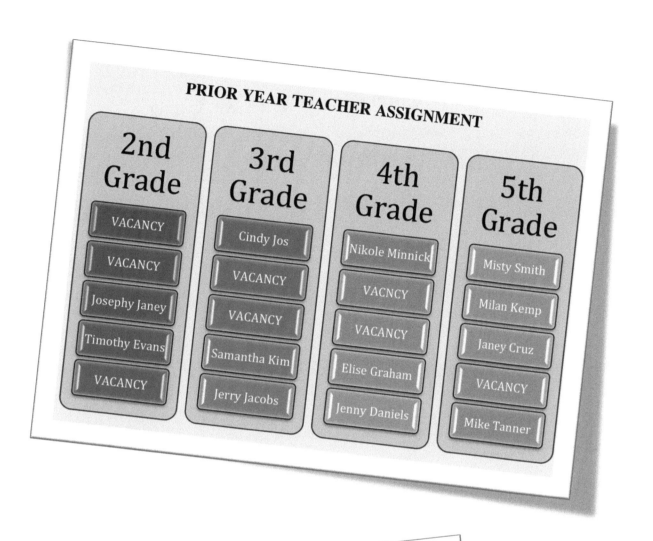

Teacher Name	I	II	III	IV	V	VI	VII	VIII
Cruz, Janey	P	P	BE	P	P	P	P	BE
Daniels, Jenny	P	P	P	P	P	BE	P	P
Evans, Timothy	U	P	P	U	U	U	P	U
Graham, Elise	P	P	P	P	P	P	P	U
Jacobs, Jerry	U	U	P	P	BE	BE	P	U
Janey, Josephy	P	P	U	P	P	P	BE	U
Jos, Cindy	BE	P	P	U	U	P	BE	U
Kemp, Milan	P	P	P	P	P	P	BE	
Kim, Samantha	P	P	BE	BE	BE	BE	BE	P
Minnick, Nikole	P	EE	EE	EE	EE	P	P	P
Smith, Misty	P	P	U	P	BE	P	P	EE
Tanner, Mike	BE	P	P	P	P	U	P	P

EE-Exceeds Expectations; P-Proficient; BE-Below Expectations; U-Unsatisfactory

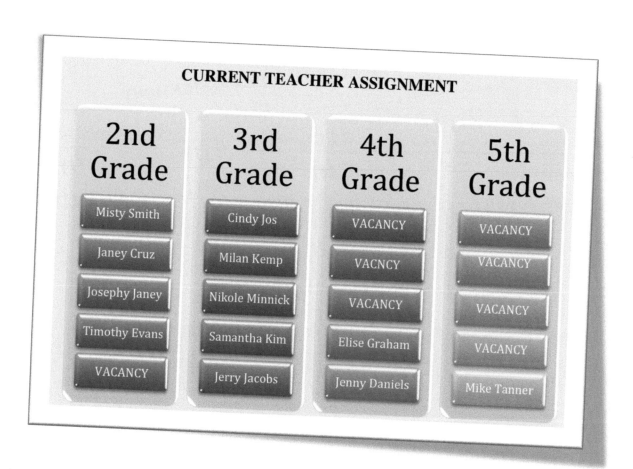

CURRENT TEACHER ASSIGNMENT

2nd Grade	3rd Grade	4th Grade	5th Grade
Misty Smith	Cindy Jos	VACANCY	VACANCY
Janey Cruz	Milan Kemp	VACNCY	VACANCY
Josephy Janey	Nikole Minnick	VACANCY	VACANCY
Timothy Evans	Samantha Kim	Elise Graham	VACANCY
VACANCY	Jerry Jacobs	Jenny Daniels	Mike Tanner

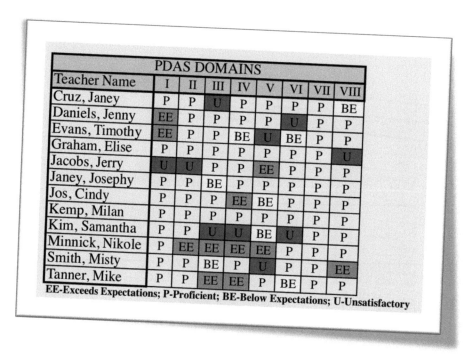

PDAS DOMAINS								
Teacher Name	I	II	III	IV	V	VI	VII	VIII
Cruz, Janey	P	P	U	P	P	P	P	BE
Daniels, Jenny	EE	P	P	P	P	U	P	P
Evans, Timothy	EE	P	P	BE	U	BE	P	P
Graham, Elise	P	P	P	P	P	P	P	U
Jacobs, Jerry	U	U	P	P	EE	P	P	P
Janey, Josephy	P	P	BE	P	P	P	P	P
Jos, Cindy	P	P	P	EE	BE	P	P	P
Kemp, Milan	P	P	P	P	P	P	P	P
Kim, Samantha	P	P	U	U	BE	U	P	P
Minnick, Nikole	P	EE	EE	EE	EE	P	P	P
Smith, Misty	P	P	BE	P	U	P	P	EE
Tanner, Mike	P	P	EE	EE	P	BE	P	P

EE-Exceeds Expectations; P-Proficient; BE-Below Expectations; U-Unsatisfactory

Teacher Name	Grade Level	# of Assigned Students
Misty Smith	2nd Grade	15
Janey Cruz	2nd Grade	12
Josephy Janey	2nd Grade	11
Timothy Evans	2nd Grade	10
VACANCY-SUB	2nd Grade	12
Cindy Jos	3rd Grade	9
Milan Kemp	3rd Grade	12
Nikole Minnick	3rd Grade	9
Samantha Kim	3rd Grade	12
Jerry Jacobs	3rd Grade	7
VACACNY-SUB	4th Grade	8
VACANCY-SUB	4th Grade	9
VACANCY-SUB	4th Grade	12
Elise Graham	4th Grade	11
Jenny Daniels	4th Grade	14
VACANCY-SUB	5th Grade	8
VACANCY-SUB	5th Grade	6
VACANCY-SUB	5th Grade	11
VACANCY-SUB	5th Grade	12
Mike Tanner	5th Grade	9

Teacher Name	Degree	Years of Teaching Experience
Cruz, Janey	B.S.	2
Daniels, Jenny	B.S.	3
Evans, Timothy	M.S.	2
Graham, Elise	M.S.	5
Jacobs, Jerry	B.S.	7
Janey, Josephy	B.S.	22
Jos, Cindy	B.S.	5
Kemp, Milan	B.S.	4
Kim, Samantha	B.S.	4
Minnick, Nikole	B.S.	2
Smith, Misty	B.S.	2
Tanner, Mike	B.S.	2

STARR LITERACY RESULTS by Teacher

	% Met Standard	% Advanced
	50	30
Cruz, Janey	59	0
Daniels, Jenny	82	5
Graham, Elise	56	0
Jacobs, Jerry	34	0
Jos, Cindy	2	0
Kemp, Milan	12	0
Kim, Samantha	77	12
Minnick, Nikole	82	15
Smith, Misty	44	0
Tanner, Mike	25	0
3rd Grade Vacancy	30	0
3rd Grade Vacancy	25	0
4th Grade Vacancy	20	0
4th Grade Vacacny	15	0
5th Grade Vacancy		

STARR MATH RESULTS by Teacher

	% Met Standard	% Advanced
	75	10
Cruz, Janey	55	0
Daniels, Jenny	70	15
Graham, Elise	55	0
Jacobs, Jerry	32	0
Jos, Cindy	20	0
Kemp, Milan	22	0
Kim, Samantha	70	18
Minnick, Nikole	76	15
Smith, Misty	55	0
Tanner, Mike	10	0
3rd Grade Vacancy	40	0
3rd Grade Vacancy	22	0
4th Grade Vacancy	23	0
4th Grade Vacacny		

Dear Principal,

I would like to schedule a meeting with you ASAP to discuss my teaching assignment for this year. I am on the only teacher in the 5th Grade-all other classrooms do not have a regular teacher assigned. I cannot teach my students because with the number of substitutes in the fifth grade wing, I find myself constantly breaking up fights and making the students follow directions. My students are suffering—HELP

Mr. Tanner

Dear Principal

Welcome! I am the most senior staff member in the building. I have seen Principals come and go in my 22 years in this school—I hope you are tough!. I am the official voice of the faculty. I would like to meet with you to share with you some of our concerns and questions about current practices.

- We need a longer lunch break
- We have too many students assigned in our classes
- We do not meet before or after school for staff development
- We need more Prep Periods
- We hope that you do not change our current lesson plan policy: teachers complete them if they wish—they are not submitted to administrators.
- We normally do not allow parents to visit—they are distractors
- We want to continue with our daily prayers morning announcements
- I always teach Kindergarten—I do not teach any other grade level

I would also like to invite you to my Church, which is the biggest church here in the town, I am one of the Assistant Ministers—We are always looking to save soles—I hope you are a GOD fearing person who believes in God. My husband also wanted me to extend an invitation to you to come and speak before the town council, he is the President.

Josephy Janey

Dear Principal

I am concerned that this is my daughter's second year being assigned to a class that does not have an assigned teacher. Why can't you get a regular teacher in the fifth grade? How will my daughter be prepared for middle school if she has had two straight years of substitutes. I want my daughter to be placed in Mr. Tanner's class immediately.

Kim Tainsly

Dear Principal

My twin girls are in the fourth grade and neither girl has been assigned to a class that has a teacher—I wan them both to be changed to a class that has a teacher. Furthermore, I want both of them to be together and I want them both to be placed in Ms. Graham's class.

Mr. and Mrs Longhornz

Dear Principal,

My son has informed me that he does not have a regular teacher assigned to his class. I find this hard to believe. He said that he has had a different substitute teacher for each day of this week. He also does not have any books and he claims that he does not have homework. Aren't the parents supposed to be made aware when there will be a substitute in the classroom for more than a month? Are the substitutes certified? What is going on in that school?

Jean Sampson

Dear Principal

I am very concerned about the number of substitutes that are in this school. I plan on attending the very next school board meeting to complain. This is just ridiculous! What is happening at this school—why aren't the teachers staying? I have also contacted CNN, NBC and ABC.

Trinete Crinkles

SUPPLEMENTARY RESOURCES
CHAPTER EIGHT
COMPETENCY SEVEN

Books

Wilmore, E. L. (2013). *Passing the Special Education TExES Exam*. Corwin Press.

Schools and Data: The Educator's Guide for Using Data to Improve Decision Making

Data Analysis for Continuous School Improvement by Bernhardt, Victoria (Oct 15, 2013)

Translating Data into Information to Improve Teaching and Learning by Bernhardt, Victoria (Sep 27, 2013)

Transformational Leadership & Decision Making in Schools by Robert E. Brower and Bradley (Brad) V. Balch (Apr 13, 2005)

Participatory Action Research for Educational Leadership: Using Data-Driven Decision Making to Improve Schools... by E. (Emily) Alana James, Margaret T. Milenkiewicz and Alan J. Bucknam (Jul 17, 2007)

The Use of Data in School Counseling: Hatching Results for Students, Programs, and the Profession by Hatch, Patricia (Trish) A. (Nov 12, 2013)

Data Driven Decisions and School Leadership by Theodore J. Kowalski, Thomas J. Lasley II and James W. Mahoney (Aug 10, 2007)

Harris, A. (2013). *Distributed school leadership: Developing tomorrow's leaders*. Routledge.

Articles
Boyd, D., Grossman, P., Ing, M., Lankford, H., Loeb, S., & Wyckoff, J. (2011). The influence of school administrators on teacher retention decisions. *American Educational Research Journal*, *48*(2), 303-333.

Lai, E. (2014). Principal leadership practices in exploiting situated possibilities to build teacher capacity for change. *Asia Pacific Education Review*, 1-11.

Major, M. L. (2013). How They Decide A Case Study Examining the Decision-Making Process for Keeping or Cutting Music in a K–12 Public School District. *Journal of Research in Music Education*, *61*(1), 5-25.

Somech, A. (2010). Participative decision making in schools: A mediating-moderating analytical framework for understanding school and teacher outcomes. *Educational Administration Quarterly*, *46*(2), 174-209.

Thoonen, E. E., Sleegers, P. J., Oort, F. J., Peetsma, T. T., & Geijsel, F. P. (2011). How to Improve Teaching Practices The Role of Teacher Motivation, Organizational Factors, and Leadership Practices. *Educational Administration Quarterly*, *47*(3), 496-536.

Websites and Blogs

http://www.schoolimprovement.com
http://www.tea.state.tx.us
http://www.corestandards.org
http://pdkintl.org/publications/kappan/
http://www.edweek.org/ew/index.html
http://www.naesp.org
http://learningforward.org/publications/learning-principal#.UxpZXxbog4M
http://www.wallacefoundation.org/Pages/default.aspx

Mini Projects/Additional Assignments

1. Develop staff development plan for teacher based on the PDAS results.
2. Develop improvement plans for teachers that received Unsatisfactory ratings on their observation.
3. Create Presentation for how your ideas for reorganization that will be presented to the teachers.
4. Create a schedule of your first 30 days—what do you plan to do.
5. Create a plan for involving a school based committee in the re-organization of the building.
6. Create a process for teachers applying for new positions within the building.
7. Create a protocol for parents' requests for having their children moved to a new classroom.

Discussion/Reflection Topics

1. "Crying is all right in its way while it lasts. But you have to stop sooner or later, and then you still have to decide what to do." — C.S. Lewis, *The Silver Chair*

2. "The hardest thing about the road not taken is that you never know where it might have led." — Lisa Wingate, *A Month of Summer*

3. "It's not hard to make decisions when you know what your values are." — Roy Disney

4. "You can't make decisions based on fear and the possibility of what might happen." — Michelle Obama

5. "Whatever you decide, don't let it be because you don't think you have a choice." Hannah Harrington

6. "If you always make the right decision, the safe decision, the one most people make, you will be the same as everyone else." — Paul Arden

7. "Jump or stay in the boat." — Margaret Stohl, *Beautiful Darkness*

8. "What is right is often forgotten by what is convenient." — Bodie Thoene

9. Inability to make decisions is one of the principal reasons executives fail. Deficiency in decision-making ranks much higher than lack of specific knowledge or technical know-how as an indicator of leadership failure--**John C. Maxwell**

10. Failures of perspective in decision-making can be due to aspects of the social utility paradox, but more often result from simple mistakes caused by inadequate thought.--**Herman Kahn**

CHAPTER 9
TeXes Principal Competency 8

(Photo: Creative Commons License USDA)

Forbes ISD
39209 Bull Market Drive
New York, TX 73203
975-833-3829
975-833-3789 (Fax)
Forbesisd.org

=======================================

Dear New Principal

It is with great pleasure that I am writing to you to confirm your appointment of Principal at Warren Buffet Elementary School. The entire school community is very excited about your appointment as they were extremely impressed with your education, skills and experience. Your strong background in finance is also a bonus as fiscal expertise will be very much needed in your role as the Principal of Buffet. One of our first priorities is regaining community confidence that sound fiscal decisions are made that are aligned with the school mission and goals to improve the education achievement of all students. As was shard with you during the interview process, Buffet has been without a strong leader for the last four years since the retirement of the Principal who served for almost four decades. This is a very small "tight-knit" community and they have not traditionally responded well to change. Collaboration and transparency will be crucial to win the support of the school community. You will be expected to provide an overview of the school budget to the members of the Chambers of Commerce in two weeks. The elders of the First Baptist Church of Forbes have also asked that you present the school budget and its alignment to the needs of the students at an open community forum they will be hosting. I strongly recommend that you become familiar with the student and faculty population and their needs. Should you need additional information, please do not hesitate to contact me.

In Continued Progress,

Andrew Carnegie

Andrew Carnegie
Superintendent

Warren Buffet Elementary School

Warren Buffet Elementary School is located in New York, TX. New York, TX is located in the geographical center of the state of Texas. It is 437 miles from the state's most westerly point on the Rio Grande River above El Paso, 412 miles from the most northerly point in the northwest corner of the Panhandle near Texline, 401 miles from the most southerly point on the Rio Grande below Brownsville and 341 miles from the most easterly point on the Sabine River near Burkeville. Maximum border-to-border distance is 801 miles from north to south and 773 miles from east to west.

Two years ago, the multinational corporation of Mars opened up a Texas Division strategically placed on the border of New York and adjacent to the town of Brady. New York is growing at an exponential pace and is equally becoming more diverse. The once blue color community is now home to over 250 Mars mid-level executives and their families. Warren Buffet is the only elementary school within 100 miles.

For this task, you will need to evaluate the growing needs of your school to create a budget that will ensure the academic and social success of all students. It is important to remember that the *Texas Principal* knows how to apply principles of effective leadership and management in relation to campus budgeting, personnel, resource utilization, financial management, and technology use. The principal knows how to:

Apply procedures for effective budget planning and management.

Work collaboratively with stakeholders to develop campus budgets.

Acquire, allocate, and manage human, material, and financial resources according to district policies and campus priorities.

Apply laws and policies to ensure sound financial management in relation to accounts, bidding, purchasing, and grants.

Use effective planning, time management, and organization of personnel to maximize attainment of district and campus goals.

Develop and implement plans for using technology and information systems to enhance school management

Accountability Rating
Met Standard

Met Standards on	Did Not Meet Standards on
- Student Achievement	- NONE
- Student Progress	
- Closing Performance Gaps	

Distinction Designation

Academic Achievement in Reading/ELA
Percent of Eligible Measures in Top Quartile
1 out of 4 = 25%
NO DISTINCTION EARNED

Academic Achievement in Mathematics
Percent of Eligible Measures in Top Quartile
0 out of 3 = 0%
NO DISTINCTION EARNED

Top 25 Percent Student Progress
NO DISTINCTION EARNED

Performance Index Report

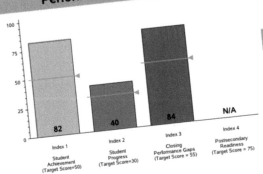

Campus Demographics

Campus Type	Elementary
Campus Size	716 Students
Grade Span	EE - 05
Percent Economically Disadvantaged	53.9%
Percent English Language Learners	23.9%
Mobility Rate	11.1%

Performance Index Summary

Index	Points Earned	Maximum Points	Index Score
1 - Student Achievement	702	858	82
2 - Student Progress	634	1,600	40
3 - Closing Performance Gaps	920	1,100	84
4 - Postsecondary Readiness	N/A	N/A	N/A

System Safeguards

Number and Percent of Indicators Met

Performance Rates	22 out of 23 = 96%
Participation Rates	14 out of 14 = 100%
Graduation Rates	N/A
Total	**36 out of 37 = 97%**

TEXAS EDUCATION AGENCY
2013 Index 1: Student Achievement Calculation Report
Warren Buffet Elementary - Forbes ISD

	All Students	African American	Hispanic	White	American Indian	Asian	Pacific Islander	Two or More Races	Special Ed	ELL
Reading										
Number of Tests	187	30	66	74	-	10	-	7	12	*
# Met or Exceeded Progress	122	18	42	49	-	8	-	5	7	*
# Exceeded Progress	37	4	11	18	-	2	-	2	3	*
% Met or Exceeded Progress	65%	60%	64%	66%	-	80%	-	71%	58%	*
% Exceeded Progress	20%	13%	17%	24%	-	20%	-	29%	25%	*
Mathematics										
Number of Tests	188	31	66	74	-	**	-	*	14	*
# Met or Exceeded Progress	101	16	38	41	-	**	-	*	5	*
# Exceeded Progress	42	5	16	18	-	**	-	*	1	*
% Met or Exceeded Progress	54%	52%	58%	55%	-	**	-	*	36%	*
% Exceeded Progress	22%	16%	24%	24%	-	**	-	*	7%	*
Writing										
Number of Tests	-	-	-	-	-	-	-	-	-	-
# Met or Exceeded Progress	-	-	-	-	-	-	-	-	-	-
# Exceeded Progress	-	-	-	-	-	-	-	-	-	-
% Met or Exceeded Progress	-	-	-	-	-	-	-	-	-	-
% Exceeded Progress	-	-	-	-	-	-	-	-	-	-

TEXAS EDUCATION AGENCY
2013 Index 1: Student Achievement Calculation Report
Warren Buffet Elementary - Forbes ISD

2013 STAAR Performance

	All Students	African American	Hispanic	White	American Indian	Asian	Pacific Islander	Two or More Races	Special Ed	Econ Disadv	ELL
All Subjects											
Percent of Tests											
% at Phase-in 1 Level II or above	82%	83%	75%	87%	-	100%	-	76%	44%	77%	59%
% at Final Level II or above	43%	35%	35%	52%	-	74%	-	40%	34%	34%	11%
% at Level III Advanced	21%	18%	17%	25%	-	47%	-	16%	5%	16%	3%
Number of Tests									0%	0%	
# at Phase-in 1 Level II or above	702	108	273	264	-	38	-	19	35	310	79
# at Final Level II or above	368	46	127	157	-	28	-	10	4	139	14
# at Level III Advanced	183	23	61	77	-	18	-	4	0	64	4
Total Tests	858	130	362	303	-	38	-	25	79	405	133
Reading											
Percent of Tests											
% at Phase-in 1 Level II or above	86%	92%	81%	89%	-	100%	-	78%	55%	82%	60%
% at Final Level II or above	49%	48%	39%	57%	-	79%	-	56%	10%	41%	13%
% at Level III Advanced	29%	25%	23%	33%	-	57%	-	33%	0%	23%	7%
Number of Tests									0%		
# at Phase-in 1 Level II or above	269	44	102	102	-	14	-	7	16	120	27
# at Final Level II or above	153	23	49	65	-	11	-	5	3	33	6
# at Level III Advanced	90	12	29	38	-	8	-	3	0		3
Total Tests	311	48	126	114	-	14	-	9	29	146	45
Mathematics											
Percent of Tests											
% at Phase-in 1 Level II or above	79%	79%	76%	80%	-	100%	-	67%	31%	76%	69%
% at Final Level II or above	37%	29%	32%	43%	-	71%	-	22%	0%	30%	11%
% at Level III Advanced	21%	19%	16%	25%	-	57%	-	11%	0%	17%	2%
Number of Tests											
# at Phase-in 1 Level II or above	245	38	96	91	-	14	-	6	9	111	31
# at Final Level II or above	115	14	40	49	-	10	-	2	0	44	5
# at Level III Advanced	66	9	20	28	-	8	-	1	0	25	1
Total Tests	311	48	126	114	-	14	-	9	29	146	45
Writing									64%	63%	42%
Percent of Tests									7%	35%	8%
% at Phase-in 1 Level II or above	75%	-	64%	89%	-	100%	-	**	0%	0%	0%
% at Final Level II or above	40%	-	34%	49%	-	60%	-	**			
% at Level III Advanced	5%	-	4%	8%	-	0%	-	**			
Number of Tests									9	30	10
# at Phase-in 1 Level II or above	81	-	34	33	-	5	-	**	1	17	2
# at Final Level II or above	43	-	18	18	-	3	-	**	0	0	0
# at Level III Advanced	5	-	2	3	-	0	-	**			
Total Tests	108	-	53	37	-	5	-	**	14	48	24

TEXAS EDUCATION AGENCY
2013 Index 1: Student Achievement Calculation Report
Warren Buffet Elementary - Forbes ISD

2013 STAAR Performance

	All Students	African American	Hispanic	White	American Indian	Asian	Pacific Islander	Two or More Races	Special Ed	Econ Disadv	ELL
Science											
Percent of Tests											
% at Phase-in 1 Level II or above	84%	81%	72%	100%	-	**	-	*	*	75%	58%
% at Final Level II or above	45%	30%	35%	66%	-	**	-	*	*	28%	5%
% at Level III Advanced	17%	7%	18%	21%	-	**	-	*	*	9%	0%
Number of Tests											
# at Phase-in 1 Level II or above	107	22	41	38	-	**	-	*	*	49	11
# at Final Level II or above	57	8	20	25	-	**	-	*	*	18	1
# at Level III Advanced	22	2	10	8	-	**	-	*	*	6	0
Total Tests	128	27	57	38	-	**	-	*	*	65	19
Social Studies											
Percent of Tests											
% at Phase-in 1 Level II or above	-	-	-	-	-	-	-	-	-	-	-
% at Final Level II or above	-	-	-	-	-	-	-	-	-	-	-
% at Level III Advanced	-	-	-	-	-	-	-	-	-	-	-
Number of Tests											
# at Phase-in 1 Level II or above	-	-	-	-	-	-	-	-	-	-	-
# at Final Level II or above	-	-	-	-	-	-	-	-	-	-	-
# at Level III Advanced	-	-	-	-	-	-	-	-	-	-	-
Total Tests	-	-	-	-	-	-	-	-	-	-	-

STAFF INFORMATION

	Campus Count	Campus Percent	Campus Group	District	State
Total Staff:	50.4	100.0%	100.0%	100.0%	100.0%
Professional Staff:	43.4	86.1%	87.0%	72.7%	63.8%
Teachers	35.8	71.0%	74.1%	57.1%	50.8%
Professional Support	4.6	9.1%	9.1%	10.7%	9.1%
Campus Admin. (School Leader.)	3.0	6.0%	3.8%	3.1%	2.9%
Educational Aides:	7.0	13.9%	13.0%	8.0%	9.1%
Total Minority Staff:	5.0	9.9%	5.1%	13.1%	44.6%
Teachers By Ethnicity and Sex:					
African American	1.0	2.8%	0.7%	1.5%	9.2%
Hispanic	2.0	5.6%	2.5%	7.3%	24.4%
White	32.8	91.6%	95.6%	89.4%	63.4%
American Indian	0.0	0.0%	0.2%	0.8%	0.4%
Asian	0.0	0.0%	0.3%	0.3%	1.3%
Pacific Islander	0.0	0.0%	0.0%	0.0%	0.1%
Two or More Races	0.0	0.0%	0.6%	0.7%	1.2%
Males	1.0	2.9%	4.0%	19.1%	23.2%
Females	34.7	97.1%	96.0%	80.9%	76.8%
Teachers by Years of Experience:					
Beginning Teachers	2.0	5.6%	1.8%	1.9%	4.6%
1-5 Years Experience	5.0	13.9%	18.9%	20.0%	28.7%
6-10 Years Experience	9.0	25.2%	24.8%	29.2%	22.3%
11-20 Years Experience	10.8	30.1%	33.8%	33.1%	26.6%
Over 20 Years Experience	9.0	25.3%	20.8%	15.8%	17.9%

	Campus	Campus Group	District	State
Average Years Experience of Teachers:	13.9 yrs.	13.4 yrs.	12.2 yrs.	11.6 yrs.
Average Years Experience of Teachers with District:	7.7 yrs.	8.4 yrs.	6.8 yrs.	8.1 yrs.
Average Teacher Salary by Years of Experience (regular duties only)				
Beginning Teachers	$46,253	$42,479	$46,337	$40,911
1-5 Years Experience	$46,898	$43,463	$47,455	$43,669
6-10 Years Experience	$48,526	$45,759	$48,612	$46,224
11-20 Years Experience	$50,994	$49,169	$51,092	$50,064
Over 20 Years Experience	$56,937	$57,928	$57,696	$58,031
Average Actual Salaries (regular duties only):				
Teachers	$51,043	$48,950	$50,589	$48,375
Professional Support	$55,815	$52,900	$57,252	$56,219
Campus Administration (School Leadership)	$61,188	$69,845	$74,978	$70,510
Contracted Instructional Staff (not incl. above):	0.0	4.1	0.0	1,645.5
Instructional Staff Percent:			72.3%	64.1%

TEXAS EDUCATION AGENCY
2013 Index 1: Student Achievement Calculation Report
Warren Buffet Elementary - Forbes ISD

ACTUAL OPERATING EXPENDITURE INFORMATION (2010-11)	Campus						Campus Group		
	General Fund	Percent	Per Student	All Funds	Percent	Per Student	All Funds	Percent	Per Student
By Function:							$123,143,189	100.0%	$6,054
Total Operating Expenditures	$3,185,920	100.0%	$6,582	$3,433,141	100.0%	$7,093	$91,853,528	74.6%	$4,515
Instruction (11,95)	$2,265,487	71.1%	$4,681	$2,357,754	68.7%	$4,871	$4,671,941	3.8%	$230
Instructional-Related Services (12,13)	$187,972	5.9%	$388	$205,091	6.0%	$424	$1,583,818	1.3%	$78
Instructional Leadership (21)	$53,630	1.7%	$111	$53,630	1.6%	$111	$8,195,824	6.7%	$403
School Leadership (23)	$235,357	7.4%	$486	$251,996	7.3%	$521	$6,111,842	5.0%	$300
Support Services-Student (31,32,33)	$262,956	8.3%	$543	$265,648	7.7%	$549	$10,726,236	8.7%	$527
Other Campus Costs (35,36,51,52,53)	$180,518	5.7%	$373	$299,022	8.7%	$618			
By Program:							$111,157,058	100.0%	$5,464
Total Operating Expenditures	$2,940,576	100.0%	$6,076	$3,032,843	100.0%	$6,266	$1,006,245	0.9%	$49
Bilingual/ESL Education (25)	$29,272	1.0%	$60	$30,170	1.0%	$62	$93,756	0.1%	$5
Career & Technical Education (22)	$0	0.0%	$0	$0	0.0%	$160	$5,535,307	5.0%	$272
Accelerated Education (24,30)	$77,177	2.6%	$159	$77,422	2.6%	$158	$1,735,076	1.6%	$85
Gifted & Talented Education (21)	$73,697	2.5%	$152	$76,389	2.5%	$4,328	$86,228,988	77.6%	$4,239
Regular Education (11)	$2,024,804	68.9%	$4,183	$2,094,652	69.1%	$1,558	$16,557,655	14.9%	$814
Special Education (23)	$735,626	25.0%	$1,520	$754,210	24.9%	$0	$0	0.0%	$0
Athletics/Related Activities (91)	$0	0.0%	$0	$0	0.0%	$0	$31	0.0%	$0
High School Allotment (31)	$0	0.0%	$0	$0	0.0%	$0	$0	0.0%	$0
Other (26,28,29)	$0	0.0%	$0	$0	0.0%	$0			

	District	State
Instructional Expenditure Ratio (11,12,13,31)	65.4%	64.8%

PROGRAM INFORMATION	Campus		Campus Group	District	State
	Count	Percent			
Student Enrollment by Program:					
Bilingual/ESL Education	8	1.5%	2.0%	6.7%	16.3%
Career & Technical Education	0	0.0%	0.0%	19.7%	21.5%
Gifted & Talented Education	32	5.9%	8.2%	6.9%	7.7%
Special Education	57	10.6%	8.2%	8.2%	8.6%
Teachers by Program (population served):					
Bilingual/ESL Education	0.5	1.4%	0.5%	1.4%	5.3%
Career & Technical Education	0.0	0.0%	0.4%	2.7%	4.1%
Compensatory Education	1.0	2.8%	2.8%	2.7%	2.9%
Gifted & Talented Education	0.5	1.4%	1.5%	1.4%	1.9%
Regular Education	28.8	80.4%	86.4%	82.6%	73.7%
Special Education	5.0	14.0%	8.4%	7.5%	8.9%
Other	0.0	0.0%	0.0%	1.8%	3.2%

'@'   Asian, Pacific Islander and Two or More Races are not available for indicators that use the former race/ethnicity definitions. See the
      Glossary for more details.
'?'   Indicates that the data for this item were statistically improbable, or were reported outside a reasonable range.
'*'   Indicates results are masked due to small numbers to protect student confidentiality.
'-'   Indicates zero observations reported for this group.
'n/a' Indicates data reporting is not applicable for this group.

Dear New Principal

I represent a cohort of parents from the Mars Company who are concerned by the lack of Gifted and Talented Programs at Buffet. It is my understanding that the current GT program is push in. We would like to meet with you to discuss the possibility of you dedicating a teacher per grade to provide GT support to our children. When we relocated to New York, we were promised by the Mayor and the Superintendent that our children would receive a top quality education; this in our eyes includes instruction that is rigorous and we are not finding that our children are currently being challenged. We have made major life adjustments in moving to this town! We have already gone to the school board and to the city council to express our concerns, we were asked to wait until you came on board to address our concerns.. Time is of the essence and we need to know when changes will take place. Please contact me ASAP so that we can arrange a meeting to discuss further.

Thank You
Dr. Jane Kingsley
(Wife of John Kinsley, Vice President-Mars Intl-Texas)

Dear New Principal

Welcome to Buffet! We are excited that you have agreed to join our team. I have been elected the spokesperson for our kindergarten team. As you aware our population is increasing monthly. The parents are asking about computers, IPADS, interactive instructional materials and updated classroom libraries. We have not purchased computer equipment in over seven years for the kindergarten classes. Our classroom libraries are comprised of donated books from the community and the church and thus are not very recent. We only have one computer per classroom and we have NO IPADS. Our parents are becoming very vocal and have actually gone to the media about this concern. Could you please arrange a time to meet with me and my team to discuss when we will be able to upgrade our technology so that we can inform our parents. They are becoming very impatient.

Thanks
Ms. Clare Jone
Room 3

Dear Principal

I am writing you to make you aware that the demographic in the building is changing. In order for us to be effective we need to have professional development activities that will help us address new student needs. Many parents want their special needs children to be mainstreamed—they do not want their children in self contained classrooms. The prior principal made every effort to mainstream the children, however very little support was provided to the teachers. In addition, instructional support is needed and remediation for students who are falling behind. We do not have enough staff to provide support, at present we are providing this support before and after school. The district has required that we all plan "think tanks" with our students; this is difficult for many of us because a large percentage of our students are unable to work independently. My understanding is that you will be presenting the budget at the First Baptist Church, many of the teachers and families are members and we would hope that you will address these concerns.

Jennfer Cameon
4th Grade Teacher

SUPPLEMENTARY RESOURCES
CHAPTER NINE
COMPETENCY EIGHT

<u>Books</u>

Vaughn, V, Sampson, Pauline and Chuck Holt (2013) Taking the Mystery Out of Texas School Finance

Wilmore, E. L. (2013). *Passing the Special Education TExES Exam*. Corwin Press.

Creighton, T. (2007). Schools and Data: The Educator's Guide for Using Data to Improve Decision Making. Corwin Press.

Data Analysis for Continuous School Improvement by Bernhardt, Victoria (Oct 15, 2013)

Translating Data into Information to Improve Teaching and Learning by Bernhardt, Victoria (Sep 27, 2013)

Articles

TEA School Funding
http://www.tea.state.tx.us/index.aspx?id=2147484908&menu_id=645&menu_id2=789&c id=2147483657

TEA Financial Accountability System Resource Guide
http://www.tea.state.tx.us/index4.aspx?id=1222

Interactive: 2014-15 School Finance Budget Viewer
by Ryan Murphy and Morgan Smith May 25, 2013
http://www.texastribune.org/library/data/83rd-sb1-school-district-funding/

Sizing Up The 2014-15 Texas Budget: Public Education Chandra Villanueva
http://forabettertexas.org/images/ED_2013_08_PP_publicedbudget.pdf

2014-2015 Budget Bill: The Job of Restoring Education Funding Remains Unfinished -
http://texasaftblog.com/hotline/?p=2998#sthash.0XoorvKc.dpuf
http://texasaftblog.com/hotline/?p=2998

Technology in Schools: The Ongoing Challenge of Access, Adequacy and Equity (NEA)
http://www.nea.org/assets/docs/PB19_Technology08.pdf

Teachers' Use of Educational Technology in U.S. Public Schools: 2009 http://nces.ed.gov/pubs2010/2010040.pdf

Websites and Blogs

www.tea.state.tx.us
www.texasisd.com/
texas.grantwatch.com/cat/9/elementary+education+grants.html
www.ed.gov/fund/landing.jhtml
www.foundationcenter.org/
texasaftblog.com/hotline/?p=2998
www.usgovernmentspending.com/us_education_spending_20.htm
http://pdkintl.org/publications/kappan/
http://www.edweek.org/ew/index.html
http://www.naesp.org

Mini Projects/Additional Assignments

1. Create a PowerPoint Presentation to the Community on the School Budget
2. Create policies for placing orders within your school.
3. Conduct GAP analysis and make recommendations for addressing deficient areas
4. Prepare a written response for each letter included in this chapter
5. Create technology plan for upgrading the use of technology in the classroom
6. Create technology plan for upgrading the use of technology by teachers
7. Create technology plan for upgrading the use of technology for daily school operations.
8. Research school grant opportunities at the local, state and federal level
9. Apply for Grant for Special School Project

Discussion/Reflection Topics

A budget tells us what we can't afford, but it doesn't keep us from buying it.
William Feather

Reforming public education, cutting property taxes, fixing adult and child protective services and funding our budget can all occur when Democrats and Republicans engage in consensus and cooperation - not cynicism and combat.
Rick Perry

We might come closer to balancing the Budget if all of us lived closer to the Commandments and the Golden Rule.
Ronald Reagan

"Don't tell me what you value, show me your budget, and I'll tell you what you value."
Joe Biden

"Claiming "the budget can't allow it" reminds me of when you walk into a restaurant at a civilized hour like ten o'clock and they say "the kitchen is closed." For years I would hear this, and think, "damn, just a little too late, oh well, thank you, I guess it's Denny's again."

And then one day it hit me: kitchens don't *close*. Just as at home, at a certain point in the night, I stop *using* the kitchen--but at three in the morning, if I want to, I still have the ability to go downstairs and "re-open" the kitchen by turning on the stove and opening the refrigerator! Restaurants are not banks; at the stroke of ten an enormous airlock doesn't seal off the kitchen and render the preparation of food an utter *impossibility.*/ No, kitchens can open and budgets are what certain people say they are."
Bill Maher

"We must consult our means rather than our wishes."
George Washington

CHAPTER 10
TeXes Principal Competency 9

(Photo: By Department of Foreign Affairs and Trade [CC-BY-2.0 (http://creativecommons.org/licenses/by/2.0)], via Wikimedia Commons)

Ancient ISD
80273 Romans Way
Ancient, TX 839273
972-372-6363
972-367-3782 (fax)
www.ancientisd.org

Dear New Principal

Welcome to Ancient ISD!!!!

We have had a whirlwind summer and as the school year is approaching we are expecting an equally tumultuous first half of the school year. Our main priority for the Donald J. Trump Elementary school will be to make sure that our community feels that our school is safe. With that being said, the first task that must be completed will be a total overhaul of our school crisis management plan. Given all of the recent school shooting, stabbings, bomb threats and emergency school closing due to inclement weather experienced by schools across the United States last year, we are in dire need of updated protocols and policies to assure our community that their children will be safe. We have a community meeting scheduled during the first week of school where you will present the Donald Trump revised and improved crisis management plan. The school board is seriously considering the possibility of school teachers being allowed to carry firearms in the school, therefore we will need for you to present a feasibility study to the board to determine if this measure will be needed given the new revised crisis management plan for your school. We must hit the ground running with this. Parents want assurances that their children will be safe and WE want them to have those assurances! Should you have questions or need further assistance please do not hesitate to contact my office.

Dr. John Wayne
Superintendent

Donald J. Trump Elementary

The town of Ancient is a fast growing family-friendly community in North Texas with a population of approximately 6,000. Ancient is located seventy five miles north of downtown Dallas in the dynamic growth area of northeast Collin County. Its close proximity to Dallas and its major thoroughfares offer easy access to all parts of the Metroplex, including Fort Worth, and other areas of Texas as well. Ancient has one elementary school and one middle school; students attend high school in the adjacent town of Tanger.

The residents of Ancient are concerned with the school district's ability to respond effectively and expeditiously to crisis that may occur at the school. Given the latest crisis experiences throughout the US in schools, parents want assurances that the school district administration are doing everything possible to put into place 21st Century polices and protocols that will keep their children safe. Your task for this case will be to put together a comprehensive Crisis Management Plan for your school. Remember, the Texas Principal knows how to apply principles of leadership and management to the campus physical plant and support systems to ensure a safe and effective learning environment. Completion of task in this case will demonstrate your understanding and master of the following:

Implement strategies that enable the school physical plant, equipment, and support systems to operate safely, efficiently, and effectively.

Apply strategies for ensuring the safety of students and personnel and for addressing emergencies and security concerns.

Develop and implement procedures for crisis planning and for responding to crises.

Apply local, state, and federal laws and policies to support sound decision-making related to school programs and operations (e.g., student services, food services, health services, transportation).

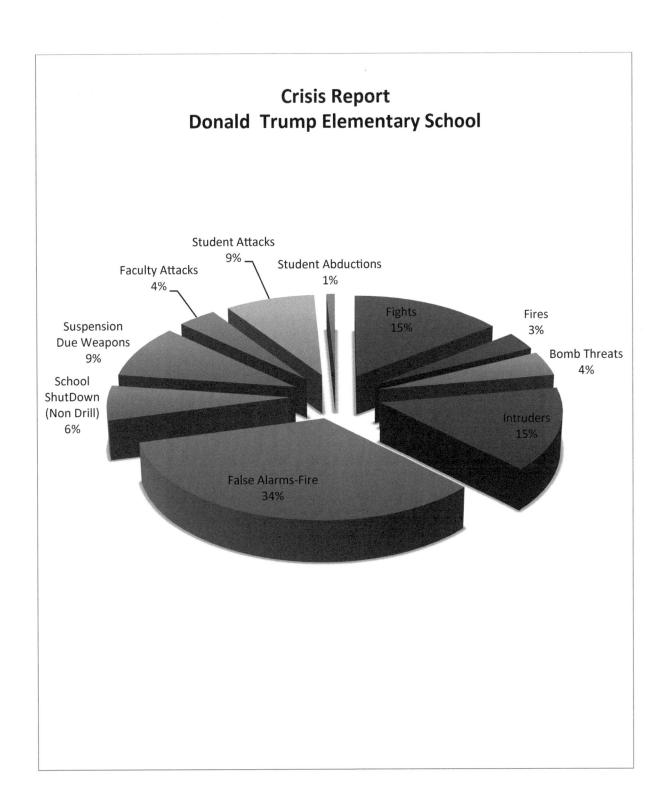

Crisis Report
Donald Trump Elementary School

Student Attacks
9%

Student Abductions
1%

Faculty Attacks
4%

Fights
15%

Fires
3%

Suspension
Due Weapons
9%

Bomb Threats
4%

School
ShutDown
(Non Drill)
6%

Intruders
15%

False Alarms-Fire
34%

Donald Trump Elementary Floor Plans

Circa 1955

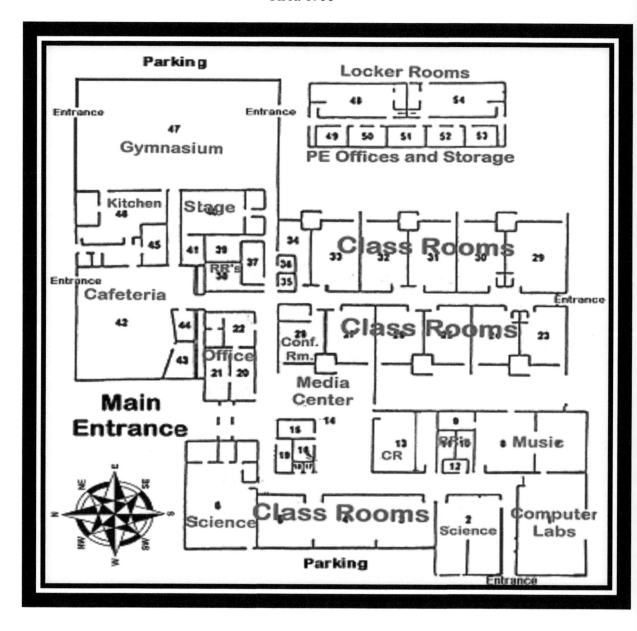

Dear Principal

I am concerned about my child's safety at school. What is the school policy on intruders—there were several school shutdowns last year and the parents were not notified. Is there a plan in place to notify parents when these emergencies occur.

Ms. Tanya Smith

Dear Principal

My name is Deara James and I have been assigned to Classroom 29. Far too often faculty or staff place a small stone in the exit door next to my classroom so that they will have easy access back into the building after they smoke their cigarettes. My pocketbook has been stolen twice and materials have been taken from my classroom. Would you please consider changing my classroom assignment?

Dear Principal

My name is Kimberly Tucker and I am assigned to work the 3rd Grade Special Needs students. My students are autistic and sudden noises and lights sets them off. Is it possible to make me aware of when there will be a fire drill or lock down drill so that I can prepare my students for the loud noises and flashing lights?

In the News…..

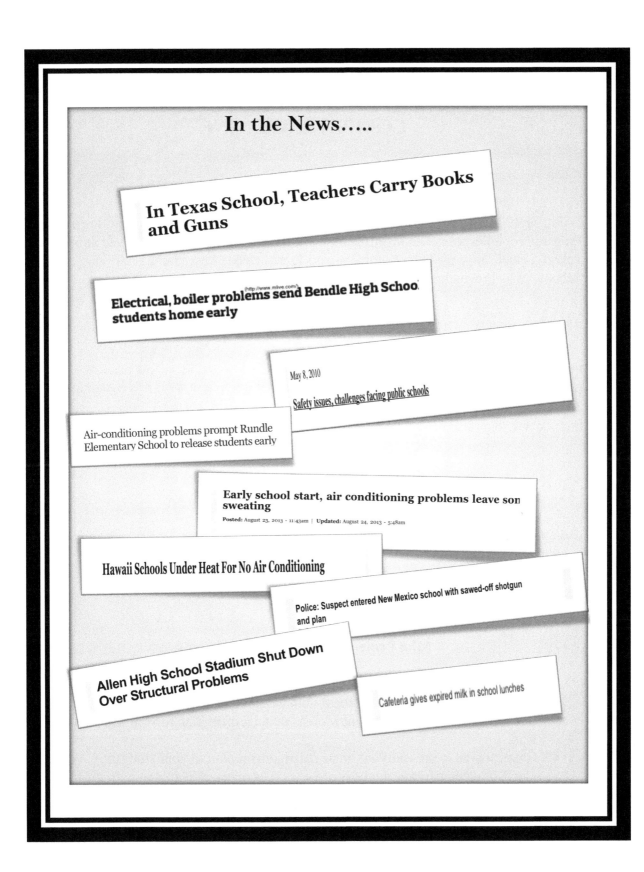

In Texas School, Teachers Carry Books and Guns

Electrical, boiler problems send Bendle High School students home early (http://www.mlive.com/)

May 8, 2010

Safety issues, challenges facing public schools

Air-conditioning problems prompt Rundle Elementary School to release students early

Early school start, air conditioning problems leave son sweating

Posted: August 23, 2013 - 11:43am | Updated: August 24, 2013 - 5:48am

Hawaii Schools Under Heat For No Air Conditioning

Police: Suspect entered New Mexico school with sawed-off shotgun and plan

Allen High School Stadium Shut Down Over Structural Problems

Cafeteria gives expired milk in school lunches

SUPPLEMENTARY RESOURCES
CHAPTER TEN
COMPETENCY NINE

Books

Wilmore, E. L. (2013). *Passing the Special Education TExES Exam*. Corwin Press.
Prepared for a Purpose: The Inspiring True Story of How One Woman Saved an Atlanta School Under Siege by Tuff, Antoinette and Tresniowski, Alex (Jan 21, 2014)
School Crisis Prevention and Intervention by Mary M. Kerr (Feb 10, 2008)

Sample Crisis Plan

http://www.cueroisd.org/userfiles/10/crisis-plan.pdf
http://www.dcschools.com/index.php?id=11
http://www.bowieisd.net/district/crisis.jsp
http://www.sonoraisd.net/DocumentCenter/Home/View/171

Websites and Blogs
http://txssc.txstate.edu
http://www2.ed.gov/admins/lead/safety/emergencyplan/index.html
http://www.dhs.gov/school-safety
www.tea.state.tx.us
www.texasisd.com/
http://pdkintl.org/publications/kappan/
http://www.edweek.org/ew/index.html
http://www.naesp.org

Mini Projects/Additional Assignments

1. Create an evacuation plan using the school floor plan provided.
2. Create a school lockdown protocol with assigned rooms
3. Create a plan to present your new crisis management plan to your teachers and staff.
4. Create a plan to present your crisis management plan to your students.
5. Conduct a comparative analysis of your crisis management plan with the crisis management plan of another school. What is similar? What is different?

Discussion/Reflection Topics
You never let a serious crisis go to waste. And what I mean by that it's an opportunity to do things you think you could not do before.

Rahm Emanuel

Effective leadership is putting first things first. Effective management is discipline, carrying it out.
Stephen Covey

Good management is the art of making problems so interesting and their solutions so constructive that everyone wants to get to work and deal with them.
Paul Hawken

The conventional definition of management is getting work done through people, but real management is developing people through work.
Agha Hasan Abedi

The most efficient way to produce anything is to bring together under one management as many as possible of the activities needed to turn out the product.
Peter Drucker

Lots of folks confuse bad management with destiny.
Kin Hubbard

I think that the best training a top manager can be engaged in is management by example.
Carlos Ghosn

The art of effective listening is essential to clear communication, and clear communication is necessary to management success.
James Cash Penney

When you think of all the conflicts we have - whether those conflicts are local, whether they are regional or global - these conflicts are often over the management, the distribution of resources. If these resources are very valuable, if these resources are scarce, if these resources are degraded, there is going to be competition.
Wangari Maathai

CHAPTER 11
Conclusions and Recommendations

The Principal is crucial to the success of any school. The Principal is charged with many responsibilities often requiring multi-tasking and immediate decision-making. Your Principal Preparation Program has provided you with a strong theoretical foundation for leading a school and this book should have provided you with the hands on experience of the practical application of those theories when applied to real life situations experienced by 21st Century School Leaders. The nine cases that are presented in this book have provided numerous opportunities for you to apply a variety of strategies for solving and/or resolving challenges demonstrating your understanding and mastery of the skills and knowledge outlined in the nine principal competencies that beginning school administrators in Texas are expected to possess.

There is NO one way to address the challenges that were presented in this book as there is NO one leadership style that will apply to every school Principal. School leadership is situational and thus appropriate responses to challenges that you will face as a school leader will be determined based on a number of factors: political climate of the school, district and community, available resources, the socio-political context of your school and community, micro and macro level impact of your decisions and legal ramifications to name a few. As a leader you must be prepared to make decisions that are in the best interest of your students, faculty and school community as defined by The State Board for Educator Certification (SBEC) in Texas and the Texas Administrative Code.

The TeXes Principal Exam 068 is a comprehensive 5-hour exam designed to measure the requisite knowledge and skills that an entry-level school administrator in Texas public schools must possess which are outlined in the nine principal competencies provided to you in this text. To successfully pass this exam on your first try you will need a strategic study plan. This exam should be taken as seriously as the certification exams that are taken by aspiring lawyers and doctors. These aspiring professionals engage in aggressive study regimes to ensure that they will pass on the first try and so should you. I recommend the following study plan:

1. Create/Join a study group with no more than five peers who are committed to mastering the techniques needed to pass this exam on the first time — no slackers!!!
2. Identify professors, peers and colleagues who can provide you with support, insight and guidance in understanding the questions on the TeXes 068 exam.
3. Purchase Passing the Principal TExES Exam Keys to Certification and School Leadership Second Edition book by Elaine Wilmore. Follow the book with fidelity.
4. Download free copy of the TeXes Principal Exam 068 Manual (http://www.texes.ets.org/assets/pdf/testprep_manuals/068_principal_82762_web.pdf). Download copies of AEIS Reports from TEA (one per person in the

166

study group)

5. Create a study calendar where you carefully plan for the review of each of the Principal Competencies. The calendar should include a minimum of one session weekly where you meet face to face or virtually (ie. Google Hangout) with all study group members to discuss and strategize answering the questions.
6. Review the Practice Questions in the Manual. Carefully dissect each question and corresponding answer options. Discuss with your study group the strategies used to answer the questions correctly always linking back to the specific language found in the corresponding Principal Competencies.
7. Discuss practice questions and answers with your professors and school administrators who can provide clarification and insight into the strategies needed for answering the questions correctly.
8. Review and discuss AEIS Reports, specifically focusing on GAP analysis and strategies that could be used to address weak areas---remember ALL children are expected the learn—ALL areas can be improved upon.
9. Attend Principal Exam Preparation Workshops/Bootcamps. Have questions handy at the workshops that you may have struggled with; seek guidance in answering the questions from the workshop facilitators.
10. Take the Practice TeXes Exam 068. Achieving a score of 80% or higher is a good indicator that you will perform well and pass the actual state test.

Many students believe that they are ready to take the Principal Exam during their last semester of their programs without having engaged in an aggressive study regime to prepare to pass the exam. As the Principal and Superintendent Certification Coordinator at my University, I am charged with providing students with clearance to take the actual TeXes Principal 068 Exam and I have had to provide repeat clearances for students who failed to pass the exam the first time. The more you familiarize yourself with the type of questions that will be asked you will begin to master strategies for answering the questions correctly. It is imperative that you are able to identify key verbs from the Principal Competencies that are embedded in the questions stems and answers: apply, develop, implement, model, establish, respond and communicate. A complete understanding of these terms will help you to strategize and identify the correct answers. Study, strategize and ask questions. Remember that your professors, peers and work colleagues should be seen as resources…seek help if you are stuck. In closing I will leave you with one of my favorite quotes:

By failing to prepare, you are preparing to fail."
— Benjamin Franklin

Dr. Kriss Kemp-Graham

ABOUT THE AUTHOR

Dr. Kemp-Graham is currently an Assistant Professor in the Department of Educational Leadership at Texas AM University-Commerce. Dr. Kemp-Graham has an undergraduate degree in Economics from the University of Pittsburgh, a Master's Degree in Urban Affairs and Planning from Hunter College in NY and a PhD in School District Administration from New York University. She currently teaches masters and doctoral level students pursuing advanced degrees in Education Administration. Dr. Kemp-Graham has worked in public education at both the central office and school level for over two decades. Her research interests include school leader cultural competence, minority female school leadership, female school leadership, middle school leadership and school leadership of "turn-around" failing schools. She believes in creating an interactive authentic environment in her classroom where students are engaged in real world experiences linking theory to practice. Dr. Kemp-Graham is a member of Delta Sigma Theta Sorority, Inc, President of Phi Delta Kappa-Commerce chapter and Coordinator of Principal Certification at her University. Dr. Kemp-Graham has been married to her best friend Derek for 18 years; they have two daughters Milan and Siobahn and two dogs Bentley and Versace.